labor of love

labor of of love

A Midwife's Memoir

CARA MUHLHAHN

PUBLISHING

New York

Copyright © 2009 Cara Muhlhahn

Published by Kaplan Publishing, a division of Kaplan, Inc.
1 Liberty Plaza, 24th Floor
New York, NY 10006

Library of Congress Cataloging-in-Publication Data
Muhlhahn, Cara.
Labor of love : a midwife's memoir / Cara Muhlhahn.
    p. cm.
ISBN 978-1-4277-9821-3 1.
Muhlhahn, Cara. 2. Midwives--New York--Biography. I. Title.
    RG950.M84 2008
    618.20092--dc22
    [B]
                                2008033507

Printed in the United States of America

10 9 8 7 6 5 4 3 2 1
ISBN-13: 978-1-4277-9821-3

Kaplan Publishing books are available at special quantity discounts to use for sales promotions, employee premiums, or educational purposes. Please email our Special Sales Department to order or for more information at kaplanpublishing@kaplan.com or write to Kaplan Publishing, 1 Liberty Plaza, 24th Floor, New York, NY 10006.

*To all the women who dare to
listen to their instincts and triumph*

CONTENTS

FOREWORD

In the spring of 2005, we were looking for homebirth midwives to interview and follow for our documentary *The Business of Being Born*. One of Abby's friends had recently delivered at home with a midwife named Cara Muhlhahn, whom she raved about.

It turned out that Abby and Cara lived only a few blocks from each other in New York City's East Village, so they met for coffee at a local café to discuss the film. Abby had never been pregnant and had met very few midwives at this point in the process.

Abby was struck by how articulately Cara described her work and her birth philosophy. She was immediately drawn in by Cara's sense of humor and open persona. Cara was downright sexy, which is not the first image that comes to mind when you say "midwife." One normally tends to picture a graying, matronly woman with loose batik clothes and Birkenstocks. But Cara not only wore low-rise jeans and high-heeled boots, but also intuitively felt like a person you could really trust and confide in — like a sister you never had. Even more impressive, she was a single mother who managed to be on call 24/7, speak three languages, and burn up the dance floor at a weekly salsa class. Was this woman for real?

Everything about her subverted the expectations and stereotypes one has of midwives. Right away, it was clear that she'd be a perfect character for our documentary. Upon returning home from the meeting, Abby called up Ricki and said, "We've found our homebirth midwife! You're going to love this woman." Thus began a relationship that has taken us on a two-year journey of filming, friendship, and many beautiful births, including Abby's own.

One of the first things you realize when talking to midwives is that each of them has a definitive story referred to as the calling. It's a moment in their lives when they discover that they need to be with women in labor and empower them to deliver their own babies. On our first interview with Cara, she described the defining moments that led up to her decision to become a midwife, which you will read about in *Labor of Love*. It is so fascinating to see how this work chose her and that she was destined to become a midwife. It's an almost spiritual calling, much like becoming an artist or a priest.

It's not a vocation that you can succeed at without passion and a calling. The demands of the profession are too intense compared to the material rewards. You have to be willing to leave your own child in order to help another woman bring her baby into the world. As a solo practitioner,

Cara has no back-up team that can swoop in for her if she has a family emergency or is feeling under the weather.

All her clients choose Cara for her unique combination of clinical skills and intuition. They build a relationship and trust with her over nine months of pregnancy. She attends each birth fulfilling the roles that four or five people might cover in a hospital setting. If the labor is five hours or thirty-five hours, Cara is there. It's an unimaginable amount of pressure and responsibility for one individual.

Beyond the crazy hours, she also has to contend with the politics that have plagued the birthing community for the past hundred years, when midwives were forced out of practice. She has to be able to work both inside and outside the system, which means finding physicians to collaborate with her if a patient develops complications or needs a cesarean section. This is no easy feat in today's litigious and fear-based birth culture. It takes a unique gift to encompass both the technical and natural worlds so seamlessly.

Watching Cara at a birth is an amazing thing. She is the epitome of grace under pressure, so intensely focused and serious about the safety of the mother and baby, while knowing exactly when to intervene and when to back away. But the most profound and moving aspect of getting to know Cara through our film is discovering the depth of her humanity and her willingness to put a client's needs above her own.

In today's system of defensive medicine, where many physicians and midwives are forced to practice as if a lawyer were looking over their shoulders, Cara operates by her own principles. She is truly an endangered breed. Our lives are richer for having known Cara. We hope that you are entertained and enlightened by her journey as much as we have been.

Abby Epstein and Ricki Lake

PROLOGUE

ON A LOW-KEY SPRING AFTERNOON, I walked my then-ten-year-old son, Liam, home from school through Tompkins Square Park in New York City's East Village.

I always look forward to this daily ritual with Liam. It's one of the few times that I get to be completely present for my kid without the distraction of my usual work demands. As a homebirth midwife in New York City, I attend up to ten births a month. So my life is highly unpredictable and forever dictated by the pager.

As Liam and I walked home together, we caught up on each other's days. He rode along beside me on his skateboard, as usual, showing me his latest tricks. We traveled through the park, past the dog run, through the basketball court, then to 11th Street, our block. Breathing in the fresh spring air added lightness to my step.

And then my pager went off.

This time it was Aileen, an illustrator and first-time mother in Brooklyn — a primipara, or "primip" in midwife-speak. Labor had started. Her doula, Jenna, was already on the way to help her navigate the early stages, when I'm not really needed. But this was the second page in the space of an hour.

I wasn't entirely surprised. First-time mothers almost always think the baby's coming sooner than it is. This is natural. It's their first time facing an incredible unknown — at once the most beautiful and most frightening event they've experienced to date. My patients, especially the primips, look to me to usher them through this unknown. To them, I am not only a midwife, but a mother who has been through what they're going through. I am their trusted guide. Even if they're just in the early stages of what we call latent labor, I often need to pay a visit and reassure them. That's the deal: if someone needs hand-holding, they get it.

Aileen paged me for a third time. When I called her, she said she had to push — a lot sooner than expected for a primip. I could sense in Aileen's voice that maybe it really was time to push. But there was also a voice in my head saying, "The shit is going to hit the fan." Later on, after one of the most challenging births in my 12 years in private practice, I will realize that this voice was right on the money.

I hurriedly called my babysitting forces into action. I have an elaborate network of sitters set up for times just like this. But no one answered. And then when I got to my car, the engine wouldn't turn over. I immediately needed alternate transportation to Brooklyn. It was time for Plan B.

I hailed a cab for Liam and me. I had never taken my son to a birth before, and had never imagined that I would.

As Liam whined about being dragged to the birth, I was torn between maternal guilt for taking him with me to work and a strong feeling that he just needed to suck it up and stop complaining. As the only medically trained person who would be at this woman's side, I needed to get there and make sure she wasn't in danger.

No one wanted to take us to Brooklyn at the height of rush hour. We got in and out of one taxi and then another. Finally, I stuffed all the cash in my pocket — about $40 — into the palm of a driver. I looked him squarely in the eye and implored him, "You have to take me to Brooklyn. Someone's life depends on it."

CHAPTER 1

A Portrait of the Midwife as a Young Girl

AS A MIDWIFE, I CAN'T RESIST starting my story with my "forelife," or my time in the womb. It's when the struggle between nature and science entered my life. I've patched the events of my forelife and birth together from stories my late mother told me and from the birth records that I sent for years ago. I was born in Englewood Hospital in New Jersey in 1957, the second of five girls. I was cared for by my great-aunt, Marie Boehme, who was a nurse at the hospital at that time.

It probably figures that I had an interesting birth. Not only did I come out breech, but I was what the doctor referred to as a crucifixion breech, which means that both of my feet came out first. In medical terms, that's probably "double footling breech." To this day, I find I tend to stand with my legs crossed at the ankles. I can't help but wonder if that's how I arrived.

According to my mom, her beloved obstetrician, Dr. Burnham, knew early on that I was breech. Every time she went to him, he would turn me around, using his hands externally on my mother's abdomen. By the next doctor's visit, though, I'd be back where I'd started, in the breech position.

In those days, breeches were delivered vaginally, even double footling breeches. Back in 1957, cesarean sections were far less common than they are today. As any midwife or obstetrician knows, it's much less risky for a baby to exit the vagina "vertex presenting," or headfirst. That's why we often try to turn breech babies. But sometimes, believe it or not, the baby knows better. In my humble opinion, I think that may have been the case with me.

My mom thought my stubborn behavior in utero attested to the irascible, inborn willfulness that she would subsequently experience through years of parenting me. One time, when I was probably 7 or 8, my sister told on me over some minor dispute. My mother called me in to be disciplined, and I refused to go because I knew I was right. She tried to lure me to her with an ice cream cone, but even then, I didn't back down.

But there's a more mechanical explanation for my breech position. A baby in utero depends on the umbilical cord to receive oxygen and nutrients. If anything constricts the flow through the cord, it could potentially interfere with growth. The doctor kept turning me around, but I must have innately known that my way was better — that when I was in the head-up position, there was a better blood flow through the cord.

There is, however, yet another theory about why I continued to assert myself in the womb. Some suggest that marital discord can cause a baby to malpresent. I have seen this in my work. When I learned, in my twenties, that my parents began marital counseling during the time I was in utero, I wondered if that stress played a role in my breech delivery.

One day a couple of years ago, as I was driving in Brooklyn, I got a call from one of my pregnant moms, Joni, who had delivered her first baby in an Oregon hospital and had chosen to have this child, her second, at home. During her first pregnancy, she had been treated for preeclampsia, a condition best described by an assortment of signs and symptoms including elevated blood pressure, swelling in the hands and face, and protein in the urine. She had been diagnosed in her previous pregnancy based on the lone symptom of higher-than-average blood pressure. If preeclampsia is left untreated, a mom could have a seizure and compromise blood flow to her baby.

Joni sounded pretty upset. She said that she felt as if she might have high blood pressure again. It was not time for our usual prenatal visit. But since I was in Brooklyn, I decided to visit her. After I arrived, the full story came out: she had discovered her husband had been cheating on her, even during this pregnancy.

Her blood pressure turned out to be fine when I measured it. She was physically okay, but in her heart, she was not. The baby, in keeping with this theory, was in a transverse, or breech, position. I related to Joni the lore about breeches being associated with marital discord, and I told her not to worry about the baby's position.

That prompted her to go with her husband to marriage counseling. In a short time, they were able to repair their relationship. Believe it or not, the baby turned around. Apparently, so did her husband. During the delivery, he went from being in the doghouse to catching his own son in the water — vertex presenting, of course. Their marriage was reborn.

My parents, however, never quite got to that point before I was born. Throughout their marriage, they were emotionally distant from each other. I adore my father and admire him in many ways. A printing industry estimator before he retired, I don't think my father ever missed a day of work. He inherited that famous German work ethic from the maternal side of his family.

From his Norwegian father, he inherited an artistic, independent, and freethinking spirit. He has always encouraged me to follow my star, but he has never been someone who easily expresses or witnesses emotion. I imagine that was hard for my mother. I know I often felt that I had to keep my emotions in check around him for fear that he might experience them as some sort of intrusion.

My parents' relationship didn't feel very cozy to me. I never sensed the warmth that I've sometimes felt between couples after they have reached a certain bond of intimacy. However, my mother later confessed that my dad was a good lover, which was nice to hear. Looking back now, I see that relative to some family cultures, ours was heated up regularly with conflict and argument. It was the classic 1950s arrangement: my mom was the homemaker and my dad the breadwinner. Since my dad was conflict-averse, that left most of the disciplining to my mom.

When pressed, my mom confessed that during her pregnancy with me, she felt my dad was less attentive to her. This is very typical of a second pregnancy. Many of my pregnant patients have a similar experience. When my mom took my dad to therapy, the subject matter never delved much deeper than the status of his favorite baseball team, the New York Mets. Of course, my dad was only in his early twenties, and this was the 1950s, before the sexual revolution. He deserved some mercy; back then, men weren't yet being encouraged to talk about their feelings.

Further testing the breech theory, I asked my father not too long ago whether there had been any kind of betrayal in he and my mom's marriage when she was carrying me. He told me there hadn't. But clearly, according to my mom, the emotional state of their union was not up to par.

My birth was no easier than my mother's pregnancy. When my mom delivered me, the entire hospital room was full of doctors-in-training observing my delivery. This might explain why she always accused me of wanting to be the center of attention. In any event, the setting was not terribly conducive to relaxing and letting it all (literally) hang out.

The birth records state that my first breath occurred at three and a half minutes after I was born. *Yikes!* I learned neonatal resuscitation in the 1980s, and at that time, there was a four-minute rule. If a baby went more than four minutes without proper oxygenation, anything from slight to serious brain injury could result. In my practice, if a baby comes out experiencing trouble breathing, I begin resuscitating immediately. Is it possible that my obstetrical forefathers did no such thing? Or do the records just fail to mention it?

MY MOM BREAST-FED ME for three months, as she did with the rest of my sisters. In those years, that was impressive. Many women in the 1950s and 1960s shunned breast-feeding altogether at the advice of their obstetricians. Some even took pills to encourage their breast milk to dry up. But my mother relied on her instincts rather than followed the prevailing medical beliefs.

Thirty-seven years later, I breast-fed my son, Liam, for two years and ten months. As a result, I believe he has my ironclad immune system, something of a family legacy. My father takes a lot of pride in having an unshakable constitution. I have almost never known him to be sick. His grandfather died at 99. A crossing guard at the time, he slipped on the ice and broke his hip. Otherwise, there's no telling how long he would have lived.

I am hardly ever sick either. Frankly, I don't have time to be. And so far, in his 12½ years, Liam has rarely been ill, either. He has not even once needed an antibiotic.

I inherited more than just quality breast milk and a steadfast immune system from my parents. They also passed down to me a belief that strongly informs my practice: nature's systems are often better than those created by humans.

My parents raised my sisters and me in New Jersey. Our town, Woodcliff Lake, was what I call countrified 'burbs, a farm town, with loamy soil, apple and peach orchards, and lots of flowering trees with intoxicating scents. Every summer, my parents would go out on their bikes and pick bushels of peaches. We'd cut them up and freeze them so we could enjoy them even in the winter months. Mom and Dad were both into gardening, and grew fruits and vegetables including strawberries, asparagus, and tomatoes on our property.

In my early years, our house was full of girls. Not only were there five in my family, but we rented out one half of our house to the Riccardos, who also had five girls, roughly the same ages as we were. We had a lot of fun, our huge pack. We stayed overnight at one another's houses, made Play-Doh peas for the plates of food that we needed for our theatrical productions of *The Sound of Music,* and went Christmas caroling around the neighborhood. We played all kinds of games, including "spies," in which we would tie each other up and pretend to torture one another. Obviously, this was before the politically correct rules about playing that are in effect today. Once, when I was 9, both families even went on vacation together to Barbados. I remember playing striptease spin-the-bottle the summer of our Barbadian vacation — with all girls, of course.

We dressed up our kittens and proudly pushed them around in a doll's baby carriage. I always had dolls to play with — from my beloved Tiny Tears, who cried "real tears," to Barbies — but they never swayed me from my tomboy roots. I loved climbing trees and catching salamanders and snakes in the glen behind our house. Still, I looked forward to having a baby of my own someday.

WE WERE RAISED WITHOUT formal religion, but my parents fostered a sense of awe for the divine powers of nature. They taught us to accept absolutely everyone, for which I am very grateful. My mother — half Italian, half Irish, and raised Catholic — turned her back on the church. She was opposed to the notion that Jews and other non-Catholics would get stuck in purgatory and never make it into heaven.

As a result, I have come to know God in my own way and on my own terms through the work I do. Day after day, I deliver babies, save lives, experience and facilitate near miracles. It would be impossible to do the work I do and not become acutely aware of the presence of... *something*. Maybe it's not an old man with a long beard or a majestic earth mother with a crown of garlands. But I get the sense that some sort of powerful "forces" out there provide order to this divine mess called life.

There wasn't a lot of structure in our house. Outside of school, our activities weren't formally scheduled. We'd just go out, on our own, and play down in the glen, until my mother would call us home for dinner. I think the fact that our free time wasn't organized helped me to develop a creative resourcefulness that complemented my personality and gave me a lot of room to grow into who I am. All in all, it was a fun-filled, wild childhood with a lot of running barefoot through the woods and streams and a lot of opportunities to use my imagination.

MY FATHER, IN PARTICULAR, had a keen appreciation of nature, and he did his best to transfer it to his five girls. A follower of Euell Gibbons, the famous naturalist who believed in living off the land and wrote *Stalking the Wild Asparagus,* my dad wanted to lead our family "back to the land." He was an adventurer who loved the outdoors and would take us camping and canoeing and fly-fishing on the Delaware River.

A true nature boy, my dad was into hydroponic gardening way before it was popular. He never let us pick pussy willows and forsythia in the spring, although everyone else picked them. His thinking was: "Why kill the plants when you can enjoy them right where they are?" He grew winter rye instead of having a lawn and pondered improvements to living, such as methane toilets. For a time, after my parents split up, he lived on his boat, a trimaran, in Seaford, Long

Island. On top, he constructed an R. Buckminster Fuller–style geodesic dome.

From a very young age, I remember my father showing me that nature was something to be respected but not feared. One night, when I was just two or three years old, I got up very late to go to the bathroom. I trucked down the very steep stairs to the downstairs bathroom. This was a big deal for me because I had bed-wetting issues until I was 9. After my great accomplishment, I froze at the bathroom's threshold. A huge daddy longlegs held me captive, leaving me no choice except to scream in terror until help arrived. My dad came down from my parents' bedroom. He put his hand down next to the daddy longlegs until it climbed up the ramp of his arm.

"See, it doesn't hurt," he said. "It's just a little daddy longlegs. It doesn't bite. There's nothing to be afraid of."

Gently releasing the creature to wander freely, my father then picked me up and took me back to bed. When I was a little older and no longer afraid, he showed me how to trap a spider under a glass without killing it: place the glass over the bug, then slide a piece of paper underneath it to contain the beast until it was safely outside. Later, in my adolescence, one of the ways I rebelled against my father was by sucking spiders up with the vacuum cleaner.

My father also helped me develop my ability to remain composed and effective in stressful situations, a quality that I began to exhibit at a young age. When I was 7, my father took my older sister and me out to sea trawling for bluefish.

My sister and I were both desperately seasick. Once we got a fish on the line, I was the one to whom my dad gave the pole. I reeled and reeled it in, in spite of the lashings that the waves were giving the boat, throwing me from side to side. The adversity of the ocean made the taste of success — and the fish — even better.

Around that same time, we were on the boat my dad kept at the 79th Street Boat Basin and I was steering. We were in the Hudson River when I spied a huge ocean liner coming up on the port side. It was passing us, but I freaked out and wanted my dad to take the helm. He gently reassured me that I could do it and guided my steering as the ship passed. I felt so accomplished afterward. My dad, the feminist. He was always letting me know I *could*. What a gift.

MY MOM WAS ALSO very supportive. Her sincerity influenced the development of that quality in my sisters and me. By nature, I'm a straight shooter, and I've found that this quality comes in handy when communicating with pregnant women. Dispensing unwelcome information about potential risks during pregnancy, labor, and childbirth can often lead to difficult moments. Telling a pregnant mom that her baby is in a breech position, for example, is always upsetting to the mom, even though she does need to know and the potential risks of the situation need to be discussed.

My mom became a mother when she was 19, and child-rearing was her primary role for many years. Years later, after my parents divorced, she went back to school to get her master's degree in English and then taught literature and writing to young men in prison — work that she loved and that demonstrated a desire to help others, which I picked up from her. She absolutely loved being a mom. It was as if she was made for motherhood. I remember that she never told negative or scary stories of childbirth, even though she delivered five children.

Mom was an amazing homemaker. She made marionettes for us for Christmas, and she handmade all of our clothes when we were very young. Pictures from my childhood years show my sisters and me dressed in beautiful matching dresses sewn by my mother. I'm almost always holding a doll. Mom passed on to us her love of sewing and crafts. I remember making lots of my own clothes, sometimes from Butterick and Simplicity patterns. It felt so good to wear something I had made. My dad was creative, too. When I was younger, he was the one who painted Easter eggs with us. Today, at 75, he is taking a woodcarving class, and makes stained-glass windows and glasses out of wine bottles.

In addition to her creative talents, Mom was a very down-to-earth, practical person. Not only would she encourage us, she would resourcefully help us devise ways to do what we wanted. I remember one winter when a group of older kids from my neighborhood had gone out sledding without me. They would not let me join because my sisters had taken out all our sleds and I didn't have one. I told Mom I was upset that I couldn't go, and she suggested I take a plastic laundry basket to the hill instead, which I very proudly did. I felt grateful not only that she came up with a solution for me, but that she helped me win victory over the mean older kids. My laundry basket turned out to be the most sought-after vehicle to take the hill in, as it went the fastest.

Mom wasn't just an efficient caretaker, she was our ally. I remember that she always encouraged us to believe in ourselves and boosted my self-esteem by encouraging independence. I never felt pressured to make choices about what I should do in life just to make my parents happy. As a teenager, I expressed a longing to learn French by living in France. My mom made no attempt to hold me back; instead she found a living situation for me there.

I respect this quality so much because I now know what can happen if children are restricted — they rebel against their parents' wishes and form an identity exclusively around the rebellion instead of around their essential selves. Mom also always respected our privacy. I remember feeling honored by that. She would never read someone's journal or mail, although she did love to read.

Despite, or in spite of, her Catholic-school upbringing, my mother had a pretty bawdy sense of humor. I'd watch W. C. Fields movies with her, and we'd both roll on the floor. She loved to tell irreverent stories about her days in school when she joined ranks with her schoolmates to pull pranks on a hard-of-hearing nun. They silently mouthed the words when they answered questions in class. The idea was to make the nun think her hearing aid was broken. She'd then turn up the volume, and the kids would scream. It sounds cruel, but in all fairness to my mom and the other kids, it seems that Catholic schools in her day were no fun and specialized in all forms of public humiliation.

I was aware that my mother was quite social and popular, although clearly she didn't have a lot of time for parties and social engagements because of her five kids. With a brood that size, she had to be quite the manager. Unfortunately for her, it was easy for us kids to push her buttons, which definitely stressed her out. In hindsight, especially now that I'm a mom (even of just one), it seems to me she was often run ragged and could have used some help.

But there was no one to help, except us, and sometimes my dad's mom, whom we called Nanager, who often came over on holidays to help out. When I was old enough, I was only too happy to help Mom with the younger kids, especially my baby sister, Ally. I was 8 years old when Allison came home from the hospital. I quickly claimed her, receiving all of the wisdom of how to care for her from my mom. I was a mom-in-training; I held her and diapered her, rocked her in her baby carriage, and calmed her in her crib. I have always had a natural connection to motherhood and babies, and I think it had a lot to do with the fact that my mom took such great pleasure in motherhood, especially the natural aspects of it. I remember being fascinated watching her breast-feed Ally in the privacy of the back stairs.

The skills that I developed by caring for my baby sister proved a worthy addition to my babysitting résumé. My first job came when I was 11, watching the kids across the street on New Year's Eve. And the jobs kept coming. That same year, I started babysitting for my seven cousins who were 10 and under. I would be diapering one, feeding another. There would be one on my hip, and I'd be disciplining the others. I didn't mind it one bit. Actually, I loved it.

I babysat reliably from age 11 to age 19 without a problem. I was a great babysitter. My mom taught me little things, like not to ever let a baby or kid be alone in the bathtub. "Never," she said. "I don't care what's going on, or if the phone rings. They could fall over and drown."

I loved that everybody felt they could trust me. It gave me great confidence that I, a self-conscious Goody Two-shoes with unfashionable eyeglasses, desperately needed.

From a very young age, when I was given responsibility, I felt like I could always handle it. It felt like an honor if someone could trust me, and that same feeling carries through to my midwifery practice today. When I have a patient who really trusts me, it means so much to me. Not all of them do. Sometimes women choose a homebirth because they think it's cool or they think they should, often without realizing the beauty of the midwifery model until the baby is safely in their arms. Regardless of where families start from, I do everything in my power to earn their trust with the highest level of clinical standards and humane care. When the baby has been delivered and the whole experience has come to a close, I say to those parents, "It means so much to me that you were able to trust my judgment completely."

It is in moments like this, when the natural expression of my attributes brings such pride and fulfillment, that I realize how grateful I am to have found my true calling.

✳

CHAPTER 2

The Wonder Years

MY TEENAGE YEARS WERE filled with many very grown-up experiences that took me beyond the limits of a typical suburban childhood and helped shape me. I learned that I could find grace under fire. If an emergency situation arose, I was able to pull myself together, take control, and keep everyone else calm, too.

The first sign of this appeared when I was in junior high. My little sister's best friend, Annie, whom I loved dearly, was hit by a car in front of our house while she was walking her dogs. The whole thing happened right before my eyes. In a matter of milliseconds, I moved from experiencing that trauma to taking charge.

I suddenly remembered some things I had learned about first aid in my seventh-grade health class. I got a blanket for Annie and said to everyone who had gathered around, "Do not move her." Then I went into the house and called an ambulance. While inside, I came across a root of some kind on a shelf in my bedroom. I decided it had magical healing "powers." I went back out to Annie and opened her hand. I put the root in it, and said, "Hold this, and everything will be okay."

And it was. For some reason, I instinctively knew how to take care of this girl both physically and emotionally, while everyone else was freaking out.

I THINK I INHERITED THAT coolheadedness from my dad. Some of it was probably passed to me genetically, and some I got from observing him. I witnessed this most profoundly when I was 14 and my family went through a truly uprooting emergency: our house burned to the ground.

I'll never forget that night in March. We had just finished tasting my dad's batch of barely mature elderberry wine. Then, my cousin Chris saw smoke barreling down the stairs from the other side of the house. Someone went upstairs for Ally, who was 6 then and already asleep.

My dad ushered every living thing out of the house, including our German shepherd, Red. The last thing he did was pick up the phone to call the fire department. Back then, you didn't just dial 911. Through the smoke, my dad had to read the number for the fire department that was written on the black, rotary wall phone. Then he quickly exited the burning house, taking the receiver with him. One of my strongest memories of that night was the vision of my father standing outside the house reporting the fire with the phone cord stretching into the burning house.

While walking away from the house, he looked through the living room window with great sadness. The two Great Bear spring water bottles, full of what had turned out to be a delicious batch of wine that resembled Port in its flavor, were now on their way to extinction, after all those months of maturing. I'm sure that for my parents, the destruction of all their worldly possessions must have been both a great loss and a huge headache. But for me, it was the beginning of an amazing adventure.

I FELT EXHILARATED by the fire. It was as if I sensed that the doors of opportunity were about to open wide as a result of this tragedy. And open they did, all the way across the Atlantic Ocean. Since we now had no place to live, my parents got the idea that it would be a good experience for us to try living in another country. They chose Spain. We traveled there on the SS *Cristoforo Colombo*. It was my first experience on an ocean liner.

Although my father went over with us, he didn't stay the whole time. He returned to the States to manage the printing business he owned and to supervise the building of our new house. We stayed in Spain with my mom, and he came to visit several times during the course of our year there. I realize now that Dad's traveling back and forth was probably a clue that their marriage was crumbling. But as a kid, I was clueless. I thought everything was peachy keen.

MY PARENTS WERE RIGHT. Living in Spain for a year was an eye-opening, life-changing experience that helped to define me. That was my first time abroad. It made me want to be not just a girl from New Jersey or America, but a woman of the world. It made me want to do work that I could do for anybody, anywhere. It made me want to learn languages — and I'm now fluent in several.

I spent my freshman year of high school living in a ten-room apartment in Alicante, Spain, that was heated by a wood-burning stove fueled with almond shells. I went to school at a small, private *academia* where I learned to speak Spanish and studied a general elementary school curriculum. There were just ten other kids in my class. The classroom culture was raucous enough to allow jeering and flying spitballs. In fact, on my first day, I was subjected to ridicule.

I had prepped vigorously the night before to be able to answer the inevitable question, *¿Como se llama?*

When *la maestra* asked me, I announced proudly, *"Yo me llamo Cara."*

The kids started cracking up. I had no idea why. It turned out that *cara* means "face" in Spanish. The kids called me *Cara dura.* Translation: "hard face," which means, "You've got a lot of nerve." But that didn't stop me from making friends. I acclimated quickly, and loved my time there. I especially liked shopping at open markets and taking siesta from 12 PM to 2 PM every day.

But after our new house was finished, it was time for us to return to New Jersey, where I would enter high school as a sophomore. I arrived home with a new sense of belonging to a community much larger than any teenage clique at Pascack Hills High School.

I think the combination of international travel and the hormonal conspiracy of my delayed entrance into womanhood made for some tough times during my teenage years. It was hard to find a comfort zone among my peers. At 16, I hadn't even gotten my period yet. I hadn't kissed boys in the Old Mill at 13 like my friends had, and I didn't have any boyfriends in high school. While my older sister Kim went on dates, I watched from the sidelines. I was different, something of a misfit.

I decided that somehow, I needed to up my coolness factor, so I tried smoking. That fascination lasted all of one puff. I decided that the price of being cool was not worth the nausea and turning green.

While my friends grooved to the latest Eagles and Allman Brothers hits, I practiced gymnastics three hours a day, rode my bike all over town, and made beautiful weavings. Like everyone did in the early to mid-1970s, some of my sisters experimented with drugs. Not me, though. While my sisters were upstairs making pot brownies, I was busy reading *The Teachings of Don Juan* by Carlos Castaneda. Everything just felt off for me in the world of drugs and rock music.

Things were not easier for my parents. Before our trip to Spain, my mom had helped our next-door neighbor gather evidence of her husband's cheating to provide grounds for divorce. Two years later, when I was 16, my own parents called it quits after 22 years of marriage. That summer, my mom sat me down and gave me the news. I don't think I cried then. I think I was probably in shock as I watched the walls of my world come crashing down. But thank god for my older sister's boyfriend, Steven, whose shoulder I later cried on.

Considering that my parents had both come from broken homes, I suppose they did pretty well by staying together as long as they had. It was an amicable divorce. I always felt that my parents loved each other enough not to trash each other in front of us kids. Most of my life, I was under the impression that my father had wanted the divorce, that he'd abandoned us, but it turns out that my mother had initiated it. Of course, it takes two to tango.

Years later, while we were on vacation together, my dad said to me, "Maybe the divorce was a mistake." That was a lot coming from a man who doesn't like to reveal himself. I interpreted his statement as a sort of apology for his part in it. I don't think I'd ever told him how much their divorce wounded me. For a long time, I don't think I actually even knew how it had affected me. But I was touched by what he said. It was very healing.

I COULDN'T WAIT TO GET OUT of New Jersey again. So my senior year of high school, I did. This time, I was off to France. I was 16 going on 17 and planned on trading in my last year of high school for a year of work overseas as an au pair. I started working for a family with two small children that ran a ski lodge in Chamrousse, near Grenoble. My many years of babysitting experience prepared me well for the simultaneous care of a newborn and a toddler. The workload was reasonable, which was important since I was already very busy trying to learn the language and culture.

As with my Spanish language immersion, I was always learning through making mistakes, which resulted in my being laughed at regularly. On one such occasion, while attempting to say *"je peux"* ("I can"), I said *"je pus"* ("I stink"). It was trial by fire, as usual.

Just as that summer and my job with the family in Chamrousse came to an end, I met a family of kids who attended the Lycée International de Saint Germain-en-Laye, a NATO school located outside of Paris. They were fluent in both French and American English. From them, I got the idea that I could both learn the language and continue my education at the same time. I decided to go there to finish high school. I sent for my school records, and the school requested proof from my mom that I was not a runaway. I got a position as a live-in au pair for a family in Versailles who knew my mother's French teacher, Cecile.

My year in France was a fantastic experience in many ways. I not only learned French but also French culture. An important phenomenon I encountered there was the less-objectified version of women. The culture was less prudish than what I had known at home. As an American teen, my experience had shown me that to be granted access to the world of feminine viability, I had to show a pass that read

"34-24-34" to the boys standing at the threshold. And those boys were the very ones who had taunted me for being flat-chested, who had told me I'd be cute "if only I had some tits," who had wondered aloud why I hadn't taken up the art of tweezing my eyebrows to improve my chances with them. In short, I found out the hard way just how hazardous American culture can be to a woman's body image. In Europe, where the feminine self was more than just a compilation of body parts, I was given the chance to regain some well needed self-confidence.

After my year at the Lycée, I paid a visit to my sister, Kim, who was living in a commune in Denmark. I was almost 18 years old. Kim and I were only 16 months apart, practically "Irish twins," as the saying goes. We had grown up sharing a room, and she had a huge influence over me. She was sexy, smart, and popular. Kim did everything before me, including discovering boys. Actually, she was well versed in boys before I ever got anywhere near them.

My mother had been very open about sex, and had taken Kim to Planned Parenthood when she got her first boyfriend. Unlike my older sister, I had been slow to mature, and had had no sexual experience. I was ready to rid myself of the status of virgin. I wanted that magic pass into womanhood as well. I think that in some way, I thought that just engaging in the sex act was the answer.

At that time, Kim was deep into personal sexual exploration. Under her leadership, we concocted a plan for me to leave my maidenhood behind. She happily — and quite swiftly, I might add — found an Irish guy to do the deed. I can't even remember his name. I don't believe I gave him cause to remember mine either. We came together exclusively for the express purpose of my deflowering. The deed was done. The next day, I don't think I felt myself transformed: just the same young woman, no longer a virgin.

AFTER I FINISHED HIGH SCHOOL, I decided to go to Montclair State College in my home state of New Jersey to study textile design. During my high school years, I had established an important relationship with my textile art teacher, Chris Martens, who had encouraged me in this field. My sister Kim had also been involved in textile design and weaving. In fact, she had originally gone to Denmark to apprentice with a famous weaver. It felt right, at the time, to develop my artistic side, a part of me that had been so influenced by my father.

While I was in college, I lived with Chris as an au pair, taking care of her boys, Andy and Erik. But after two years of textile art at Montclair State, I felt unfulfilled. I didn't know why I was studying what I was studying. I also experienced my first bouts of anorexia, something I would struggle with only into my early twenties. Fortunately, I pretty quickly outgrew it.

As much as I loved my studies in textile art, I didn't feel deeply satisfied. One day I was sitting alone at the loom weaving a beautiful piece of green and beige fabric I had designed, I had a meditative epiphany. I thought: *I do not exist to make art to be displayed in galleries for people to come and see.*

I was realizing that I wanted to help others concretely, person to person, face to face. To me, the idea of "helping" others by exposing them to my concept of beauty felt empty and narcissistic.

That simple awareness became the underlying impetus of my return to France and my subsequent trip to Morocco. There I would stumble upon another realization about my career aspirations. Perhaps it came from being in a developing country, feeling culturally alienated, and longing for a unity of mankind, but something deep within me insisted on finding some kind of work that would be relevant throughout time, from life in caves through life in outer space. I didn't know yet that I wanted to be a midwife. I just knew that one of the criteria for my career was that it did not feature built-in obsolescence. Furthermore, to satisfy my innate sense of humanity, my career path had to be free from the potential for economic or cultural discrimination.

Refining these realizations into concrete plans would have me busy for years in a process that involved separating as-yet-undefined wheat from chaff. I traveled all of the roads I had a need to explore, then matched my discoveries to the blueprint of my soul's design. Although I consider myself to have a pretty good analytical mind, I have never come to find my direction through deductive reasoning. The inspiration and driving force behind so many of the things I have achieved has come from a deep inner truth that I slowly uncovered with each life experience. I had to travel through Europe and Morocco before I unearthed a desire to work in the medical field, and only later would I discover my desire to be a midwife.

SO, AT AGE 19, I wasn't sure yet what I wanted to do with my life, but I was ready to leave New Jersey again. I wanted to see more of the world. I asked my father whether he thought I should stick with school or travel, and he said, "Go and travel. You'll get a better education that way." His response seems remarkable to me now. How many fathers would tell their daughters to do that?

He was right. I spent the next 14 months "vagabonding" around Europe, and it informed my life in more ways than I can count. I started off back in France. I worked picking grapes at Les Vendanges, the annual grape-harvest ritual, and house-sat in the mountains of Les Cevennes. While living there, a woman across the hills had a homebirth. That was probably the first time I'd been that close to a baby being born.

Next, I was off to Morocco, which was a very different experience. Morocco was where I had to talk myself out of many challenging and potentially risky situations. One time, I was hitchhiking back to Agadir, where I lived in an adobed-over cave built by a fisherman on a sand cliff. I was picked up by a truck driver. He made a crude gesture and propositioned me: *"Nique-nique, madame?"*

After some quick thinking, I replied in French "In your country, you are allowed to have many wives, and in mine only one." I lied and told him I was married. Imagine his surprise when he realized that not every female American tourist he saw was "free" and available for the picking. After that, he shook my hand and dropped me off at my destination.

I had a very profound experience in Morocco that I believe was the first important step on the path toward my eventual career. A man knocked on the door of my cave dwelling in the middle of the night. He said a butane camping stove had exploded and the force had knocked a girl 17 feet onto a rock jetty. He wanted to know if we had a car to drive her to the hospital. Of course, we didn't.

There we were, unable to do anything for this girl. I was haunted by the fact that I was present and yet completely impotent. I couldn't save her. The girl died. I thought that if only I had a car or knew CPR, I could have made a difference. That experience carved my relationship with the world. I thought, *Next time, I'm going to be the one who can do something.*

Something, but what exactly?

I MADE A SHORT TRIP to Denmark to visit my sister Kim. This time, we discussed my career prospects. We talked late into the night about my aspirations. I knew I wanted to be in a medical, helping profession, but I didn't know what my particular angle should be.

I'm pretty sure Kim is the one who threw out the word *midwife.* In 1970s Denmark, a country in which most children were delivered with the help of a midwife for centuries, a midwife was a pretty great thing to be. Midwives there have always represented the cream of the crop, intellectually and in terms of social prestige, even more so than doctors. She suggested I look into it once I was back in the States. Finally, the fit felt right and I decided to proceed with the pursuit of a career in midwifery.

＊

CHAPTER 3

Blood, Sweat, and Tears

AT 19, I REMEMBER feeling like it had taken me *so long* to figure out what to do with my life. Now, looking back, I realize that 19 wasn't late at all. And to think, my mother had gotten married at that incredibly innocent age.

After my visit with Kim, I arrived back in New Jersey. Right away, I set about making money for my future endeavors. After a brief period of research, I somehow "caught the drift," to use 1970s parlance, that the best place to study midwifery was on the West Coast. Once I knew what I wanted to do, I was able to trust whatever was going to take me toward that. At my core, I have always had faith that once I clearly see my vision, it will manifest. It would just take a little elbow grease. Or, maybe, a lot.

One day, on the subway in New York City, I noticed a guy who seemed to be about my age. We both had backpacks.

We started talking, and he mentioned that a friend of his had an extra seat on a Learjet that would be flying to Portland, Oregon. I knew midwifery was happening in Portland. And that I had to get there.

So I flew to Oregon on that Learjet knowing neither the guy who offered me the ticket nor anybody out there. I had no job or an apartment lined up. But I had been traveling off the cuff for years. I didn't need to know how success would be built, just that it would be. My instincts had always either served me well or taught me a much-needed lesson, even in distant countries and in foreign languages. I'm good at moving fast and without question when my gut tells me where I should be. This may be one of the key personality traits that makes me right for midwifery.

So there I was in Corvallis, Oregon. I stayed a couple of nights with the guy who brought me there on the plane. Then I answered a room-for-rent ad on a bulletin board and moved into a young couple's house. After I got settled, I went to a meeting of a group called HOME, which I believe stood for Home-Oriented Maternity Experience. There was a group of pregnant couples, and then me, a 19-year-old quasi-maiden.

The midwife introduced herself, and then we proceeded around the room and did the same. Everyone else talked about how they were planning on having their baby at home. And then it was my turn. I felt quite intimidated and uncomfortable next to all of these ripe peaches. I was so young, with so little experience as a woman.

I had only recently gotten my period. When it hadn't arrived by age 16, my mom took me to Columbia Presbyterian Medical Center in New York City, and a gynecologist there put me on the pill. The pill gave me a simulated cycle for a year, but I didn't like the side effects, so I went off it when I was 17. It took another two years for me to bleed on my own.

Finally, my turn came to introduce myself at the HOME meeting. Swimming in self-consciousness, but very on the spot, I said, very plainly, "I'm Cara, and I want to be a midwife."

The midwife, Johanna, called me the very next day, and invited me to begin an apprenticeship with her. Johanna lived in the beautiful hills of Oregon, about 45 minutes outside of Corvallis. The room I rented was nearby, and I joined the community garden. I was situated, but hardly ready for my first call when it came. Of course it came in the middle of the night. And, of course, it was the mother's second baby; second babies always come fast.

I valiantly rode across town on my bicycle. The mother was quite active when I arrived. I called Johanna, and she told me to boil some water to sterilize the instruments. Today, we generally sterilize them at home in the oven before coming to the birth. Johanna assured me she'd be on her way.

I went into the bedroom to see the mom. She was on her hands and knees, a position many women would naturally assume to give birth if left to their own devices. A close friend of hers had come to offer support. The friend was stressed about the fact that the midwife hadn't yet arrived. She was hyped up, screaming, "It's coming, it's *coming*!" She was doing a good job of freaking out the birthing mom. I had never attended a birth before, but I immediately knew the friend had to go.

I found serenity within myself—the same serenity I found in junior high after my sister's friend was hit by a car. I calmly asked her friend to leave the room, which she promptly did.

The baby's head was visible at the perineum. I said to the mother, "Everything is going to be okay. I've got the water boiling. Johanna's on her way. You're going to be fine." Even though I had never attended a birth before, somehow, I found the right words to reassure the birthing mom.

Johanna made it just in time, though I now know that the baby could have been born without any assistance. In any case, the experience was thrilling for me. That night, I knew without question that I had come to the right place.

It didn't hurt that Oregon was so beautiful. Johanna held prenatal visits at her country house. I would ride out there on a motorcycle. The setting was calm, fun, and woman-centered in a way that helped to create an optimistic, kind atmosphere toward the impending birth.

I WORKED WITH JOHANNA for six months. As much as I was learning, it soon became evident that something was missing. In every setting I've worked in, the missing piece has quickly become obvious to me, which then made continuing there for much longer an impossibility. I discovered what that piece was in Oregon when Johanna and I were at a birth that was not going well. The baby's head was out, but that was all. The baby was turning blue. Johanna yelled, "Call 911!" and I remember thinking, *911 my ass! Shouldn't we be getting that baby out?*

Although Johanna was a registered nurse, or RN, she was a lay midwife who hadn't been through any sort of midwifery education. She liked doing births, and she liked doing hospice. I've heard that's the way it is for some midwives — they like to be there, ushering people as comfortably as possible through both life portals, birth and death. It has always just been about birth for me, although I was the one to help my mother through her dying moments in March of 1998. I found the words then, as well. I sang "Danny Boy" to her, as she had to me many bedtimes as a child, completely unaware that it was Saint Patrick's Day, until after her final exhale when the song "Danny Boy" came on the radio, giving meaning to my intense grief.

Eventually, another emergency occurred in Johanna's practice, and again, we were unequipped to handle it. I knew I'd learned all I could there. Apprenticing with Johanna had been a great introduction, but I was realizing that I needed a more formal education. I needed to move on and study elsewhere.

I began to explore additional learning options. I soon found out about a lay midwifery clinic and birthing center in the Texas border town of El Paso. So I made that my next destination, and headed south on a 60-hour Greyhound bus trip to take part in the program. It involved living and working in the birthing center, where many Mexican women came to the United States to have their babies, often to facilitate legal immigration.

Melinda's maternity center attracted aspiring midwives from all over. At that time, there were women from British Columbia, Colorado, Vermont, New Jersey (that would be me), and many other places. My time there was great; it was like a huge slumber party with a mission. Many of us lived at the center, because that was the most affordable option.

To supplement my meager income, once a week I donated my blood to a blood bank for money. My education was important to me, and I was willing to make all kinds of sacrifices for it. Could there be a more perfect metaphor than giving your own blood for a profession that demands everything from those who enter it?

Melinda's center was great. I learned so much. The population was about 85 to 90 percent Mexican, so the Spanish I'd learned while living in Spain came in handy. All of the women walked throughout their labor, as the birthing rooms were like delivery rooms and the mothers couldn't be admitted into those rooms until they were ready to birth.

Melinda's place was top notch. She was, and still is, the vision of competence. Her place is where I learned excellent clinical midwifery, including how to coach a woman giving birth to a breech. For a healthy birth, the cervix had to be 11 centimeters. Normally, 10 is considered fully dilated, but with a breech, extra room is needed because the larger part — the head — is coming later and could potentially get stuck if the cervix isn't open enough. Each time a woman delivering breech felt the urge to push, I had to coax her to breathe instead of push. That way, nothing she or I would do could get in the way of the body's wisdom.

At Melinda's, I also learned that fundal pressure, when used with discretion, can provide a safer alternative to assisted delivery with forceps or vacuum extraction, the current trend. Using her hands, the midwife applies pressure externally to the fundus — the top of the uterus — while the woman is bearing down. Usually when one mentions the words "fundal pressure," more than a few eyebrows rise. But countless birth practitioners have used it at one time or another, including ob-gyns in hospitals, even after the advent of forceps and vacuum-assisted delivery. I have never, in more than 30 years of practicing midwifery, seen fundal pressure cause a problem.

Melinda's birthing center was where I witnessed how calling on higher forces can be instrumental in moving things forward. For those who don't believe in god or even "the powers that be," you can chalk it up to the sheer will of intention or the placebo effect of faith. But something else was often at work there, especially at difficult moments. There were times during a long or difficult birth when a Mexican husband would be down on his knees in prayer in the birth room, and somehow, suddenly, everything would work out fine. The beauty and humility of those prayers have never left me. Nor has the awareness that I am reckoning with a design not of my own making.

Ironically, though, Melinda's was also the place where I learned that hospitals can be very necessary and where I felt, for the second time, that I wanted to possess more clinical skills so as to be better prepared. One experience in particular pretty much clinched it.

A mother was hemorrhaging postpartum. We had to transfer her to a hospital as soon as possible. We got in the car, and I was told to pinch her nipples and keep her talking so that she wouldn't lose consciousness. When they received her at the hospital, she had a blood pressure of 40 over "palp," or 0. I instinctively knew that this mother needed to have an IV to give her blood volume, but as lay midwives, we couldn't do that. Once again, I knew that there was probably more that I could have done to help the situation, given the right training. That night I told myself, *I'm going to have more skills and knowledge at my disposal than pinching a woman's nipples in an emergency.*

During my time in El Paso, I attended a hearing at the Department of Health. A homebirth midwife was being implicated in a maternal death. That was another pivotal moment for me. I knew that if I never wanted to be in that position — accused and unprotected — I could help it. That's not to say that this mother died as a result of malpractice. I didn't know the circumstances. But I was learning that I wanted to have as much clinical training and knowledge as possible, so I could significantly lower the risks for babies, mothers, and myself. I started thinking about how to get the kind of education that would make me feel good about doing this work for the rest of my life.

The next logical turn in my story might seem to be evident. One could assume that I would have taken the observations and experiences I had gleaned so far to heart and eagerly begun pursuing the next level of my education. But my quest for that fulfillment would be postponed for a couple of years. Apparently I had some more chaff to process.

AS WITH MANY A WEARY traveler, it started with one simple misstep: a long layover in San Francisco between buses. I was traveling north from Texas to my former home of Oregon. What better place than San Francisco to be stuck with a long wait? I decided to take a tour of Fisherman's Wharf.

It was on this very trip that the Moonies caught me in their web. First there was an invitation to dinner. Then there was a follow-up invitation to a pilot project farm outside of town. There, all kinds of socially innovative solutions to economic inequities were being explored. One such program had food from the farm being trucked into warehouses staffed by members of an economic underclass, who received homegrown vittles in exchange for their work. This was the 1970s! Change could come! Idealism reigned! So why not get involved?

It happened almost imperceptibly. The coercion, like any kind of brainwashing, was subtle at first. It was very powerful. And I was not alone. My generation, which had matured at the tail end of the 1960s and the beginning of the 1970s, was looking beyond the nuclear family for fulfillment. Hence the emergence of communes, such as The Farm in Tennessee, where legendary midwife Ina May Gaskin still lives and practices today. When I was recruited, I was searching. So there I was, 22 years old and a new member of Reverend Sun Myung Moon's Unification Church. Yes, I was a "Moonie."

But important issues such as feeding the poor soon became eclipsed by the spiritual agenda of a misguided messiah, as Reverend Moon believed himself to be. To solve humankind's larger woes, he professed to be gathering disciples willing to pay off "the indemnity," or spiritual debt, of humankind. According to him, each person was saddled with some amount of it, and we all carried a portion of the "collective sin." The Reverend Moon had an easy solution for working it off or "buying salvation": fundraising for him.

Okay, okay, I know. Hell, I hadn't even been raised to believe in original sin.

Suffice it to say, I possessed certain vulnerabilities that made me a ready target. I was far from my roots and my home, and having traveled the world, I was open to new and unfamiliar experiences. At the invitation dinner, there is no reference to Moonies or the unification church. In fact, the identity is disguised until three weeks into "learning" about the community's values, which on the surface are presented as those of a Christian community working to better society. The new recruits are only privy to the soft side. Only later, after you've agreed to study the teachings, are you made aware that the divine principle is the book of Reverend Moon's Unification Church.

I traveled around the West for two years, working hard at raising money for the church. I was on a "travel team." We'd drive around in a little van, and then we'd jump out and sell jewelry door-to-door. I was fully prepared to take part in Reverend Moon's mass arranged marriage at Madison Square Garden. Then I was kidnapped.

I had set up a meeting with my parents who lived in New Jersey to introduce them to my future husband, a fellow Moonie. That was their only shot to rescue me, and they took it. My parents had hired two deprogrammers. At my parents' bidding, two hefty deprogrammers kidnapped me on the streets of New York City. They got there just in time, which turned out to be just as well for my "fiancé," who confessed he had been wishing for a Japanese wife. They took me to a safe house where I stayed for a few weeks. I was sequestered in an upstairs room. They wouldn't let me out, except to talk to me in the kitchen about the contradictions in Reverend Moon's reworkings of biblical texts. I didn't give them a hard time. I think I was relieved and ready to be deprogrammed. A few years later, one of those deprogrammers was on trial for kidnapping a cult member across state lines. I testified on his behalf and helped to win the case.

As a parent myself now, I understand that it must have been a difficult and painful decision for my parents to make.

They chose to forcibly remove their daughter, a young adult in her early twenties, from a "religious pursuit" of her own choosing. And I sure am glad they did.

✳

CHAPTER 4

School Days

AFTER MY LITTLE two-year derailment, I was ready to pursue midwifery from a new perspective. Before my time with the Moonies, I had learned all I could from informal apprenticeships. I was ready for serious study in an institution of learning. I decided to study nursing as a first step to becoming a certified nurse midwife.

Once I got back home, I began taking premed science classes at Lehman College within the City University of New York (CUNY) system. My plan was to finish my prerequisites there and then transfer to Columbia University for my nursing degree.

During my studies, I had the pleasure of living with Golda and Willi Kessler, an older couple, in the Riverdale section of the Bronx. Chris Martens, my high school textile arts teacher, helped me get a position as a home attendant with them. Willi had been struck with Alzheimer's. I took him for walks and helped Golda care for him in his graceful descent.

They were a lovely couple with a beautiful story. Willi was born Catholic and German. Golda was Jewish and German. They lived together in France during the Resistance. During that time, Golda gave birth to their only son. She delivered in a convent after riding there on her bicycle while in labor! Willi risked his life on a regular basis by smuggling food to his Jewish friends. He was a noble man, and still was, even with Alzheimer's.

I took Willi for walks around the quiet back streets of Riverdale. As we walked, I kept an eye on him to make sure he didn't get lost. When he heard a car, he would usher me out of harm's way over to the side of the road, shuffling all the way. He never even realized that I was there to protect *him*. He just kept looking out for others.

Willi spoke to me in German. Sometimes he thought I was Golda. He loved her very much. Witnessing Golda watch Willi slowly lose his powers was a painful yet genuine experience. She would read letters from friends reporting the loss of another member of their peer group, and I watched the reality of old age spread out before me. Golda taught me with the wisdom and grit she had developed throughout the course of her life. I felt grateful to have experience as my teacher.

Golda eventually had to put Willi in a home, where we visited him on a regular basis. Watching Alzheimer's claim Willi taught me something very important: this illness seemed to remove the socialization skills one had learned through life, revealing the golden (as in Willi's case) or not-so-golden character within. It showed me that in the end, a person's façade would be swept away, revealing the true nature of the soul. This realization made me commit even more firmly to pursuing my work as a midwife, to doing work that I believed really mattered.

THROUGH ALL THIS, I WAS busy at Lehman College, taking my prerequisites for nursing school. I was at the top of my class there, and ranked number one in premed chemistry. My biology teacher asked me about my plans. I told him I wanted to become a nurse so I could become a midwife. He told me he was concerned that I would be bored with nursing. Why didn't I consider becoming a doctor of osteopathy? He could even help me get into a good program. The implication of his comment was that I was too intelligent to be a nurse or midwife. It's ironic, because in Danish society, midwives are the ones with the best grades. They are more highly revered than doctors.

My biology teacher tried on the cap of guidance counselor and suggested I become a dentist. I wondered why, as I had never expressed the slightest degree of interest in shiny whites or cavity-free living. His reply just blew my mind.

He said, "Dentists have great hours. And they almost never get sued." I remember thinking, *This is my guidance counselor to hell!* He didn't understand what made me tick on any level. I was not about to pick a profession based exclusively on convenience or the level of legal liability.

Around that time, I also attended Physicians for Social Responsibility meetings. Several medical students tried to talk me into becoming a physician, saying that my perspective was really needed in that field. I had a moment of doubt about my aspirations: Why was everyone trying to steer me away from my passion?

I considered medical school. Ultimately, though, I didn't do it. For one thing, I was paying for my education myself. Where was I going to get the money for this even more expensive education with no income? On another level, I think that after having been subjected to the coercion inherent in the socialization process of cult living, I couldn't willingly consent to the equally powerful socialization process of medical school and residency.

Years later, when I was a nurse at Columbia Presbyterian Medical Center, I thanked god that I had not made the decision to become a doctor. We frequently saw the attending or a tired chief resident torture the intern dog of the day during board turnover. A hazing I was grateful to do without. I looked on with disapproval at this reigning reality, much as a child might become wary of a teacher who shut down a child's enthusiasm for learning with insensitive displays of public humiliation.

In the end, I traded eight to ten years of character-warping educational methods, power, money, and a place at the top for the preservation of my democratic soul. The price might appear big to others, but I have no regrets! The integrity of my ideals was strengthened many times over as a result of making conscious commitments to humane values. The decision to remain on my own path, no matter how lacking in status, was another polishing of one facet of the diamond.

Aside from the practicalities that kept me from medical school, something else helped quell my confusion and re-clarify my aspirations. I participated in a "shadow" program at North Central Bronx Hospital, where I followed the mid-wives on their rounds to see what real practice was about. The incomparable Mae Chin was often my mentor there. Many famous and very powerful midwives have run the North Central Bronx Midwifery Service, Mae Chin among them. This was my first exposure to hospital midwifery. I was coming from lay midwifery in Oregon and Texas to an inner-city hospital with a medically underserved population, where the midwifery care was being run by nurse mid-wives. They were in complete control. When I witnessed them "giving report" in the morning, it seemed to me that they were very smart and conscientious.

Mae was very supportive of my shadowing. She liked that I had been a lay midwife before. She didn't in any way discriminate against me for that, as do some nurse midwives when they encounter lay midwives. In fact, she let me do an exam on a woman who was breech, showing me the feet in the lower uterine segment.

Having her take me into her confidence like that was a highlight, and a small omen that I was indeed going in the right direction. I had a great experience at North Central

Bronx Hospital. The midwives there were — and still are — a very empowered group. I was so impressed with this midwifery-run service, I knew that I would not be bored in the field.

AT AGE 25, GETTING MY nursing degree was next on my agenda. I was afraid I wouldn't be able to afford Columbia, since I had no money, but I scraped it together, through Pell grants, a scholarship from the Leopold Schepp Foundation, and work study.

My transfer to Columbia reminded me of how it feels to move from a small town to a big city. At Lehman, I had been a star student. Teachers there would sit down with me and get involved in my future and my success. I was a much smaller fish in a much bigger pond at Columbia. Without connections, anonymity came at a high price, too. Aside from the cost of tuition and books, I had to pay to use a campus typewriter to type my papers: 25 cents for every 15 minutes. If I ran out of coins, the typewriter would just quit while I was in the middle of a major paper. This was the early 1980s — no one had personal computers yet.

Still, I made the dean's list. And in time, I discovered some extremely riveting and caring teachers there. I found people to study with, especially my new best friend, Barbara. We made it through the rigorous program together.

I met another key friend there, too. His name was Mauro, and he was my first true guy friend. He became my first male confidant. I felt comfortable enough with him to talk about girl stuff, like my period.

Up to that point, I had only gotten to know men through dating and had always been kind of wary of them. I suppose it came from growing up with only girls in our house. I just did not know how to relate to men at all.

Actually, Mauro would have made a great first boyfriend for me. He was a truly wonderful man. I don't know whether he had sisters, but I think he must have because he wasn't uncomfortable around women like I was around men. I thought that we were just going to be friends, and if it was ever going to be more, we'd take it one step at a time.

But we never moved our relationship to a romantic level. I'm still not sure why. Maybe it was because my parents had gotten divorced. Maybe it was because my dad wasn't that attentive of a father. I think for sure it was because I was a late bloomer and that made things complicated for me, hormonally and socially. I was embarrassed that I wasn't "normal," that I wasn't dating like all the other girls.

Mauro gave me an important and lasting gift: an introduction to Jungian therapy. I had started flirting with it while I was in college, but it wasn't until I was in my thirties that I started going to therapy regularly. It has been an incredible, fortuitous journey.

I was attracted to Jungian therapy for many reasons, the first of which was that Mauro introduced me to it. That he did it made it feel approachable to me. I also liked that interpreting dreams was a big part of it, a less confrontational way of getting at emotional wounds. I probably knew instinctively that I would try to skirt those. I liked the fact that I might reveal myself through a dream, in spite of my more conscious attempts not to confront an issue. I did a lot of dream work in the beginning and loved it.

Jungian therapy is not focused on "fixing" or changing anyone. It encourages you to discover all the parts of the self, including the darker aspects, or the components of your "shadow." Once each is identified, you are supposed to embrace them and become wholly, uniquely yourself. In many ways, I have felt "different" all my life, and like a misfit in many situations. I remember in particular a comment made by another female high school student, when I chose to travel abroad during my senior year; she wondered why I would miss the prom! The process of individuation I went through as an adult has helped me give voice and lend validity to the many different parts of myself that society may have told me were not welcome.

Many women of my generation chose motherhood as a path, before career pursuits. I never felt at home with that choice, and because of that felt a bit out of sync with my peers. Therapy has helped me to incorporate those parts in fulfilling what I feel is my divine blueprint, my purpose in life, and my unique approach to living.

While I was at Columbia, I still lived in the Riverdale apartment that Golda had rented to me. New York was different then. It was not nearly as safe as it has become. One night, while walking home from school around 10 PM through Ewing Park in Riverdale, I was attacked at gun-point. In that section of the park, it is easy to see from one side to the other; I never feared making that crossing and, in fact, always enjoyed having a moment for a brief encounter with nature.

That night, halfway across the 50-yard path, someone emerged from behind some trees. I knew right away that something was not right. My instincts were right on. When the guy came up to me and asked me the time, I knew I was in trouble. Before I had a chance to run away, the guy grabbed my right arm and stuck a gun to my ribs.

"What do you want?" I begged him. I'd have gladly given up my wallet to save my life.

"Get in the park!" he ordered. I didn't like this. I knew that if he wanted to rob me, we didn't need to go anywhere. My feet froze to the ground, and I heard a voice in my head. This one was different from the intuitive voice that always guides me. This one was as distinct as the night was dark. It told me, *The gun is a prop.*

I had never seen a gun before, prop or otherwise. This one was doing a very effective job of scaring me nearly to death. But the voice gave me courage. My attacker lifted the gun to my temple and instructed, "Get in the park or I'll kill you." I decided to risk all and fight. Why? I suppose I couldn't take dying terrified. I figured that if I were going to die anyway, I would die on the offensive, not as a victim begging for my life. He started hitting me with the gun. I'd never studied kung fu, but I swear, anyone who saw me that night would think that I had. I was surprised at how easily I blocked each swipe of the gun to my head. It's amazing what the body does under the influence of adrenaline!

Something occurred to me. Why was he hitting me with the gun instead of shooting me? I let out an incredible scream, the kind I always hoped would come out of me when I needed it. A man opened his apartment window and offered words of hope. "Hey, lady," he called down, "I called the police!" Confronted with this news, my attacker hightailed it out of there.

I found out afterward that my internal voice had not only given me the courage to fight. It had also given me correct information. The attacker later stopped a nurse at the bus stop on her way to work the night shift at Memorial Sloan Kettering. Our stories crossed at the Bronx Sex Crimes Unit. This brave woman had wrestled the gun from the perp's hand and tried to use it against him. But it didn't work. The gun *was* a prop. *Whoa.*

That was my closest brush with death. And yet I survived, in spite of not following the standard advice given out by rape experts. Was it true grit? God's will? Dumb luck? Whatever it was, some voice had wanted me to continue living. I knew that I had received a gift, completely unsolicited. It came at the right time. Little did I know, I would need an injection of warrior glory to help soften the injustices to be found right around the corner. The idealism I'd developed in my adolescence was about to be put to the test.

THE FIRST CHALLENGE CAME during my nurse externship program at Columbia. Classes were out for the summer, and I was gaining experience working on a thoracic and abdominal surgery floor.

I was well loved and respected there. I, a mere student, had found a woman, who'd recently had coronary artery bypass grafting surgery, cyanotic (turning blue) and had basically saved her life. But even though people raved about my work, I still seemed to attract more attention for my differentness.

That differentness revealed itself in many ways. Sometimes I would bring in a guitar to sing to a homeless man on the ward of whom I was particularly fond. I made a beautiful poster to hang on the wall to help the staff with Spanish-speaking patients. The poster, fashioned after a Matisse paper cutout called *Young Woman in Blue*, was a quick reference for the names of the body parts in Spanish. I had cut letters out of the blue leg so that the word *pierna* remained on the thigh of the blue leg, in white. It was beautiful, and the staff felt honored that I had made them that present.

But that didn't keep the nurse administrator from calling me into the office one day to discuss how "unprofessional" it was of me to sing in the hallways or to my patients. I was stung. If I was foulmouthed or uncaring, I could see taking me to task. But singing as I worked? Making artwork to give staff a symbolic leg up with communication? *Please!*

Something rose up inside me that made me able to stand up for myself. Very respectfully but firmly, I said to the nurse administrator, "I don't understand how you, who are overweight and a smoker, can call me unprofessional, since your behavior clearly doesn't show these patients a good example." To this day, I wonder where I got the *cojones* to say such a thing. But I knew I was right. And she backed off.

Back at school, I'd soon face a different kind of moral challenge. I was sick one day. Even though I'm the kind of person who doesn't get sick, every so often some crazy New York bug goes around that no one — not even me — can avoid. I was running a fever and feeling just awful, so I didn't go to school.

The problem was, there was a class that day that every student *had* to attend. Being absent wasn't an option, no matter how high the fever. Unbeknownst to me, my friend Barbara signed me into the class even though I wasn't there. I didn't ask her to do that, but she thought she was saving my ass. We were the best of friends, like two peas in a pod. We always had each other's back.

The teacher reviewed the list and then noticed that I wasn't there. She called me up at home and asked me why I was signed in if I wasn't there. I wasn't terribly concerned. I was always most comfortable with the truth. I told her I was sick, and unbeknownst to me, someone must have signed me in. She asked me who it was. I told her I didn't know, which was true.

Much later that day, my friend Barb told me she had done it. The next day, when the teacher asked again who it was, I wouldn't tell. Although at that point I did know, I held out. I didn't think it was right to rat out someone who had been innocently trying to protect me.

I was punished. The administration tried to make me out as a liar. They said, "Maybe you'll lie about narcotics." They actually made me cry. But they misconstrued the whole thing. I was simply defending a friend who had acted out of a noble sentiment. I was not going to let her down. And I wasn't going to conform to their ideas of what determined whether I was good or not.

The punishment for my crime was to write a paper. I turned it into a manifesto. I wrote about stages in moral development, specifically primitive morality based on tribe, family, or culturally agreed-upon values versus the morality of the conscience. And I talked about where the nursing profession at large was in terms of morality. It was my way of saying, *Fuck you, because I did the right thing.*

I'm glad I stuck to my guns. I'm very proud of my loyalty and of that side of myself that has a higher sense of justice that doesn't always jibe with institutional rules. I paid a price for that. They could have failed me. But they didn't. I graduated with honors. And went on to face even bigger moral challenges.

✳

CHAPTER 5

Truth and Consequences

I FELT QUITE ACCOMPLISHED when I graduated with a BS in nursing from Columbia. My mom, dad, and Golda were all there to celebrate on the big day. Golda had become one of my surrogate parents. She had helped me grow from an ex-cult member to a grounded, functional, achieving member of society. Her influence was important in my life.

For the next ten years, I would learn the ropes in hospitals and birthing centers. When I was fresh out of school, I heard that it would be difficult for a new grad to get a job in labor and delivery, or L&D. But I didn't want to spend any more time doing another kind of nursing. That would only add time to my journey toward midwifery.

My first job out of nursing school was at Long Island College Hospital (LICH) in Brooklyn. They took new grads in L&D. I found a sublet in Brooklyn Heights on Joralemon Street, over a firehouse. My apartment was just within walking distance of the hospital. It was a good job. I liked all the doctors and the nurses, and I loved the work. I knew that I was acquiring skills I would need far into the future, such as starting IVs. I was beginning to learn how to distinguish the normal from the pathological. Plus, I had my first salaried professional job, and it felt great. I had made it. I had arrived in the adult world.

While I was working there, I began pursuing another passion in my spare time. A longtime lover of jazz music, especially old standards, I began to study singing. Some of this interest was inherited from my dad. He'd named my sister Laura after a jazz standard of the same name. My dad would always sing off-key, "Laura ... is the face on the passing train..." During my jazz-singing days, I learned that my dad had loved the version of that song done by Charlie Parker with strings.

A famous bebop pianist and composer named Barry Harris ran evening workshops in Manhattan at the Jazz Cultural Theatre, and I began attending them.

I loved singing, and I was pretty good at it. I have a deep, dusky alto voice and a fairly good range. By singing old standards, like "Love Me or Leave Me" and "East of the Sun," I was able to experiment with and express my rhythmic, lyrical nature. Though I loved it, I soon realized how much I still had to learn at Barry's workshop. The format for learning was that Barry would accompany the singer on the piano along with a rhythm section of his choosing, usually drum and bass students who were already gigging. I never knew how lucky I was back then; today, he rarely accompanies the singers in class. Each singer could sing two songs and then the kind and forgiving but ever-so-real Barry, or "Professor Bop" as we called him, would give us feedback and constructive criticism.

I'll never forget my first time singing on a stage in public. I was so nervous. The whole way through the song, I snapped my fingers on the 1 and 3. Barry was in the back of the room snapping on the 2 and 4, trying to clue me in. I didn't get it until the song was over, probably because I was just waiting for it to be over. Things got progressively better, though, as my performance anxiety decreased. Barry worked his magic on me as he did, and still does, on many aspiring jazz musicians.

Singing for me wasn't about creating a sultry diva image. What I was really trying to do was to experience a place completely inside the time, a place that musicians are always working toward finding. I practiced a lot to that end and found it on occasion. In that place, each person is an integral part of the larger whole. The song then carries the singer along inside it and brings with it incomparable feelings of ecstasy. Music can really be like a drug but with less serious side effects than most other consciousness-altering substances.

I loved the society of the deep-feeling aesthetes that I found among my new musician friends. Their philosophies were the same as mine: A person's value was not defined by physical attractiveness and money. Young and old, all were welcome to try their hand at creating beauty. Opportunity was open to all. All one needed was the $7 Barry charged, a meager fee he was kind enough to maintain so that his instruction wasn't limited to the financially well-endowed. My heart opened like a flower. All that singing about romance and love was something of an aphrodisiac. I guess falling for Ronnen, a beautiful and soulful jazz guitarist, was an understandable next step.

Ronnen was Israeli. He had come to New York especially to study jazz with Barry, who attracts many international students to his program. Ronnen was the youngest of seven children and very attached to his family. Around the time that I had been working in labor and delivery at LICH for a year, he needed to go back to Israel for a while to visit his beloved family and invited me to go with him. I was thrilled. I was so in love, there was no question that I would go with him. Plus, there is that part of me that is forever a traveler. I realized I could always get another job as a nurse. I quit labor and delivery at LICH and headed for the Holy Land with Ronnen.

We lived together in Israel for six magnificent months. We stayed with his family and performed together in nightclubs and *kibbutzim* all around the country. I was singing jazz with my beautiful soulful boyfriend! It was an exciting, creative time.

While it provided room and board, staying with his family also posed certain challenges. I loved Ronnen's family, especially his mom. She was more lovingly referred to as *safta,* the Hebrew word for "grandma," as she was a grand-mother many times over already. She and I would speak to each other in French, as she was of Tunisian origin. The whole family was warm and welcoming. And they loved me, too. But they were very traditional. His mother had trouble seeing Ronnen's pursuit of music as a career having any serious possibilities. She even laughed at it. I got it. This woman had lost her first-born in a cave in the mountains of Tunis while fleeing the Germans in World War II. She'd suffered the ravages of war, poverty, and immigration so that her son would not. I knew I could love her.

Ronnen and I were not allowed to have sex in their apartment, out of respect for his mom. It didn't matter to her that we were already a very solid couple and very much in love. We weren't married, and — the bigger issue — I wasn't Jewish.

At first I didn't realize how insurmountable an obstacle that was. In hindsight, I probably would have converted for Ronnen, if I knew that would have saved our relationship. I did everything short of that. I learned Hebrew rather quickly, although never to the extent that I had learned French or Spanish, which were easier for me. I fasted with the family on Yom Kippur. But the long and short of it was that his family, as much as they loved me, couldn't come to terms with the idea of Ronnen marrying a non-Jew.

I was crushed. My heart was much bigger than all the rules, and I didn't understand why it wasn't that way for other people. We were a great couple. Unfortunately, his family's views ultimately undermined our relationship.

Ironically, our next step was marriage. But it wasn't the kind of marriage I was looking for. It was all business. Ronnen needed a green card to come back to the States. He wanted to study some more with Barry Harris. We flew to Cyprus, where a Jew and non-Jew could be married without question, and sealed the deal. We kept it a secret so that we wouldn't upset his beloved *safta*.

I was very wary of a green-card marriage. I was uncomfortable making that kind of a legal statement without first making the very necessary commitment of the heart. I had never faked anything in my life. And shortly before we left Israel, things got further complicated. I got pregnant.

I knew from the moment that I was pregnant that Ronnen wasn't ready to have that baby. The last thing I had ever wanted was to force a guy's hand in that particular way. When we returned to New York, I set off on the very difficult inner journey toward making the right decision. Would I have the baby or not? It is a journey that, in many parts of the world, women don't have the option to take.

I hadn't been doing regular therapy sessions for a while, but I called up my old Jungian therapist for a crisis session. We talked dreams. I kept having dreams about medical instruments inside my body. *No! I did not want that!*

I was torn, but I decided not to go through with the pregnancy. I made the appointment for a termination. The night before the abortion, I prepared for the next day. I said goodbye, in my heart, to the tiny fetus that I was carrying.

Then, in the middle of the night, I woke up with contractions that were four minutes apart. After about four hours of what felt like labor, a little egg-shaped sac fell out of me. It had an embryo inside. I saved it for days in the fridge until the odor of its decomposition prompted me to dispose of it.

Although I had ultimately decided to go ahead with the abortion, in the end, I hadn't needed to. While some might feel that it was simply a coincidental miscarriage, I felt that I had had some sort of psychic abortion. It seemed odd that the miscarriage happened only after I was finally able to take responsibility for what I had decided and was able to say goodbye.

I wasn't racked with guilt, although there was some, because I had consciously decided not to let this child live. That seems like a lot of power. Maybe it was too much. Over the years, I have certainly questioned the rightness of my decision.

For me, the subject of abortion is a lot like that of pain medications for labor. I don't want to take away a woman's choice to take pain medications. They are available to her, and I have administered them. But I do know that most women will feel better after delivery if they haven't had the meds. Similarly with abortion, while I am pro-choice and chose an abortion, myself, there can be spiritual or physical regrets that one isn't aware of until after the fact. I almost wish that I might not have exercised that right. Oftentimes, especially when unplanned pregnancy renders us frightened and confused, we can't see how things might change, possibly for the better, down the line. To this day, I wonder what might have happened if I had had the child that Ronnen wasn't ready for. I know that I'm sorry, in a way, that I had the power to terminate. I know he was a boy, just as I knew that my son, Liam, was a boy even before I got the amniocentesis results, revealing his gender.

RONNEN AND I CONTINUED living together and loving each other for a while longer. I got a job at Columbia Presbyterian Medical Center in labor and delivery. Ronnen and I had an apartment, conveniently, a few blocks from there. We were very close, yet I felt a shift in our relationship. His mom had said that she would jump out of a window if he had kids with me. I think he just couldn't deal with the pressure of her disapproval.

After four years together, my first love and I broke up. Once we were over, Ronnen went on to date mostly Jewish girls, and eventually we ended our green-card marriage with a divorce so that he could marry a Jewish woman. It broke my heart.

Today, Ronnen and I hear about each other mostly through his nephew, Ilan, who is now Liam's piano teacher. Ilan had the courage to marry a non-Jewish woman he loved, and I salute him. He had been in the house the day that Ronnen had been admonished by his older brother Jeudah. Ilan was nine when Jeudah had told Ronnen not to break his mother's heart by having children with me. Apparently, that had a powerful effect on him.

A couple of years ago, I learned Ilan was considering whether to marry his girlfriend, Lauren. I said, "Ilan, don't make the same mistake Ronnen did."

He told me, "Don't worry, I already told my parents that I am marrying Lauren. If they're not comfortable with it, too bad." His dad is Jeudah, the same big brother who had intervened in Ronnen's life to protect his mom's deepest wishes.

When I heard of Ilan's decision, I cried. It was sad to me that Ronnen had not possessed the same amount of courage. I think I only realized at that moment that it might have been possible for Ronnen to have done the same thing for me so many years ago. In a strange way, I felt healed by his nephew's personal courage.

✳

CHAPTER 6

Institutional Agendas

ROM AGE 27 TO 32, I worked at Columbia Presbyterian, and I spent some of those years at Columbia's Allen Pavilion. In my spare time, I was still seriously pursuing singing. I sang at jazz cafés in the evenings. It was a great creative outlet for me. There were times when I even thought of pursuing a singing career.

But after a time, I came to realize that my heart is in service, not performance, just as I had realized long ago that weaving, although a talent of mine, was not where my heart was. Performance is not what makes me tick, not my heart and soul. So I kept music as my hobby.

At Columbia Presbyterian, I learned a lot and had many good experiences. Nurses practically ran the labor and delivery unit. We were a smart, assertive group of women. There, I met Miriam Schwarzchild, a great midwife who is now a dear friend and colleague. She helped me deliver Liam.

We now work closely together and cover each other when we need to.

But I also saw a lot of things at the hospital that really disturbed me. I will go so far as to say that, in my opinion, women were regularly unknowingly violated. Oh the things I've witnessed!

One time, a patient's labor had stalled. I asked the obstetrical resident whether it was okay for the patient to get out of the bed and squat. This resident was known for her sense of humor. She had joked that when she was pregnant, she was going to get her epidural at eight months. The resident said to the patient, "Oh yeah, you can do that jungle stuff if you want to." Funny maybe, but not terribly encouraging. Naturally, not much squatting went on that night. None. No standing, either. That patient wound up with a C-section.

Some doctors just can't make birth happen fast enough — even the births that are likely to be pretty swift on their own. One woman who came in while in labor never even got the option of a single push! It was her tenth child. The doctor examined her and then announced, "Okay, you're fully dilated. Get the vacuum." For her *tenth* child, this doctor was using vacuum extraction! Nine kids had already come through this woman's pelvis. She probably didn't even have to push at that point. It would have been a very fast delivery without the vacuum. *Ay ay ay!*

There was another troubling incident with a multip, or multipara, a woman who's already given birth at least once.

This doctor instructed a resident to use forceps on the baby. Now, multips have very fast second deliveries. The baby moves down through the pelvis much more quickly. After the mother feels the need to push, the baby is usually out within about 30 minutes or less. Those mothers rarely need coaching, and forceps are almost never used to get the baby out.

But the resident employed the forceps because he was learning how to use them in delivery. Columbia Presbyterian is a teaching hospital, and often, patients are part of the learning process. But they never explained to the birthing woman, "We're doing this partly for instructional purposes — you are taking part in that." In my practice, I keep my patients informed, and I involve them in all of the choices. But in this case, they just went ahead and did what they wanted. To me, this felt like a deception on top of a violation.

I got very upset about the whole thing, and it was hard for me to contain my emotions. That heightened sense of justice of mine, the one that doesn't always jibe with the institutional agenda and makes it hard for me to keep my mouth shut? It reared its head. I huffed at the doctor, "I'd like to see you do that to your wife!" I couldn't help myself. I wound up getting reprimanded for being "insubordinate."

FORTUNATELY, I FOUND A MORE constructive way to deal with my frustration over the way doctors and residents were doing things and what I still believe were narrow, misguided views. I researched the points I felt strongest about making and wrote the information on index cards, which I would carry with me. When a situation would arise where the residents were doing things I thought were counterintuitive, I would whip out the cards.

For example, one day a mother was at a certain point in her labor and I thought it would be good for her to stand up. A resident said to me very matter-of-factly, "No, we really can't stand her up." I responded, "Really? Because according to a study done by Caldeyro-Barcia in Uruguay in 1961, standing women up actually shortens labor by about 78 minutes in primips," and handed him the card with the details.

I felt the index cards gave me new credibility. The doctors and residents were probably rolling their eyes inside. But residents and nurses are often supportive of one another, since we work so closely together in the stressful environment of the labor room. I know that they respected my need to search for understanding and to back it up with studies. That fostered good relationships, some of which continue to this day. For instance, I met Dr. Jacques Moritz when he was a resident at Columbia. He is an obstetrician and gynecologist who refers patients to me all the time. Our friendship and collegiality has persisted for more than 20 years.

Not all personalities can withstand excessive amounts of stress without warping in an unfavorable way. One attending at Columbia Presbyterian was particularly haughty and high strung. A lot of adrenaline goes along with obstetrics, so there are a lot of type-A people in the field. One time, we were doing a cesarean section. It was an emergency, and we had to get the baby out right away because of fetal distress. At that time, Columbia Presbyterian was known for its ability to deliver babies in six minutes or less. There was a certain machismo about that among the staff, and it was a well-deserved machismo. When a baby needs to be saved in an emergency situation, it's imperative that it can be done quickly, and well.

I was the scrub nurse for that C-section. The scrub nurse hands the doctor the tools. It had been a tense operation, and the doctor was cranky and bossy, which was not really unusual for her. After the surgery was done and the baby was fine, she continued barking at me in a harsh tone. Fortunately, by this time, I had learned not to react emotionally.

I turned to her calmly and said, "Doctor, the baby is out, and she's fine. The conditions have been downgraded from urgent to nonurgent." It actually helped her adjust down a bit. I guess I've learned how to be a walking tranquilizer, which isn't a bad thing.

In all fairness, I can understand where the barking comes from in an emergency situation. In my own practice, although I am generally able to remain composed and in good spirits, sometimes things can get hairy. In those cases, I will say to the mother and the doula, and whoever else is there, "Listen, I might bark a little, because we've got to get this baby out. I apologize in advance."

Not long ago, a mother was delivering at home. The baby was having a heart-rate deceleration, an indication to me that the cord might be around the baby's neck. I had to get this mother to stand between contractions as a way to make sure the baby could recapture its much-needed oxygen and reverse the deceleration. I communicated that to the doula. Instead of working with me when I asked her to get the mother up, she felt sorry for her. She tried to advocate for her by saying how hard it would be for the mother to stand.

Afterward, I had a talk with the doula. I said, "If you're going to work with me, you have to be her ally and my accomplice at the same time." Most of the time, though, there's never really a good excuse for harsh tones at a birth.

AFTER A WHILE, I MOVED over to Columbia Presbyterian's Allen Pavilion. It was a newer community hospital located at 225th and Broadway, just up the street from the main hospital. They had a midwifery-run service there. There were no residents, except for those who were on-call for cesarean sections. There was no anesthesia department. And in the beginning, there were no patients. We were the pioneers who agreed to work there.

I was excited about the change. I didn't know yet that I was about to receive a cosmic kick in the pants. Every now and then, life will hand me one of those. Facing me with some horrible humiliation or other formidable challenge, it will cause me to question who and what I am. Most of the time, though, instead of scaring me away from my vision, it redirects me back to my true path. It reminds me of why I chose what I do and emboldens me to recommit.

While I'm going through the experience, however, all I know is that it sucks and I feel wronged. But then it all passes, and in time, my situation ultimately changes for the better. When I reflect back, it seems as if forces had actually been conspiring, if somewhat ungracefully, to deliver me to my right place. After enough of these cosmic kicks in the pants, I have come to realize that sometimes not getting what I think I want is a blessing.

I had been very valued at Babies Hospital 12 South, the labor and delivery ward at Columbia Presbyterian. When I moved over to Allen Pavilion, it was partly with the goal of becoming a charge nurse, as was suggested by my nurse administrator. Although the position was clinically pretty much the same as the one I had been in, I would be floor manager. There would also be a slightly higher salary and more prestige. I thought I wanted this position more than anything. It seemed as if I was being groomed for it. People told me they thought I was perfect for the job. I was really responsible and well respected as a great clinician. When I interviewed, though, I didn't get the job.

Apparently, a whole crew of nurses had come en masse from Albert Einstein Medical Center in the Bronx and scooped up all of the charge positions. Columbia must have felt that it needed a change of guard for political reasons or something else I was unaware of. I was devastated. It was hard for me to get over.

I had really settled into nursing at that point. I wasn't even thinking about going to midwifery school. In a way, I was getting complacent. I had a salary and worked my shifts, but I still had a life. Not getting the charge nurse job woke me up, though.

Miriam had gone to the State University of New York at Downstate Medical Center for a year of midwifery school. She loved the experience, and she kept encouraging me to go. Shortly after I didn't get the charge nurse job, I applied. I got in, and that got me back on my right path.

That's not to say that I have any regrets about having spent five years in labor and delivery at a hospital. I learned so much there. So many midwives don't want to become nurses first. They want to skip that experience, and I can understand why. But I feel that what I learned in those five years undoubtedly helped me become a better midwife and a better clinician. I am now an authority on why it's better in many cases to deliver at home.

I realized soon afterward that if I had gotten the charge nurse job, I might never have left Columbia Presbyterian or the nursing field. I would have gotten caught up in the hierarchy and lost touch with the part of my soul that knew it was time to move on to a different kind of education. I might never have moved beyond my nursing job to the wonderful, more autonomous, and more clinically challenging professional niche I have carved out for myself as a professional midwife.

I WENT THROUGH THE year-long midwifery program at SUNY Downstate in Brooklyn. As part of the program, I did an "integration," which is like a mini-residency for mid-wives. I was placed at the Maternity Center, the first birth center in Manhattan, at 92nd and Madison. SUNY Downstate was a wonderful program with great clinical sites. The teachers there worked very hard to make our learning fun and to cater to each person's individual style. The program provided me with many opportunities to observe what went on in labor and delivery suites in quite a few hospitals, among them Kings County, Downstate, and Metropolitan.

Kings County was a true city hospital, all grit and no frills. One experience I observed there made my hair stand on end. A drug-addicted mom came into the labor and delivery triage area. She was as high as a kite. The chief resident was called to come and deal with her. I put the fetal heart rate monitor on the baby, and it was low, in the 60s. (It should be somewhere between 120 and 160.) I kept telling the doctor how low it was, and he kept asking her what drugs she was taking. This went on for a good ten minutes or more — precious minutes with a low fetal heart rate like that.

The doctor wouldn't move to do a C-section until she gave him the information. I know that he needed to know what drugs she was taking so that he could administer a safe dose of anesthesia. But it was clear that this woman was not going to deliver that information. She wasn't going to say, "I've taken two Tylenol, one Advil, and one pipeful of crack."

I couldn't help feeling that he was wasting time. Apparently he couldn't bring himself to care about this drug addict or the kid she might be bringing into the world. Maybe he thought, *That kid's going to be so neurologically damaged anyway.* To me, it looked as though he wrote her and her child's safety off because of her drug addiction. Maybe he assumed that she didn't care enough about her baby not to be an addict in the first place, so he decided he didn't care, either. Finally, he stat-sectioned her. He made a judgment call about how to give her anesthesia without the information about the drugs she had taken. But it was too late. The baby was dead.

There are bad doctors, and there are good doctors. Good doctors can be found in all the city's hospitals. For example, I first met the perinatologist Dr. Franz Margono, who currently does any necessary antepartum testing for my patients, during his residency at Kings County Hospital. Not every obstetrician is willing to work with midwives, but he is, perhaps because he trained at SUNY Downstate, where midwifery students were trained. Every homebirth midwife who works with him appreciates his excellent knowledge base, clinical expertise, and professional humility.

WHILE I STUDIED AT SUNY DOWNSTATE, I lived in Gravesend, Brooklyn, where all the Italian guys had their own little gardens on two-by-four foot patches of dirt. There, I also got to show off my gardening skills. In the back of the house I was living in was a huge lot. I asked my landlord, "Would you like me to plant a garden?" He said sure. Then he tried to get me to use Miracle Grow. I was like, "Miracle Grow? Are you kidding? I'll just put horse shit in the dirt, then wait for some rain and some sunshine to make things grow."

So I made this gorgeous garden that I actually covered in brown plastic instead of mulch. I made holes for the seedlings, and then I never had to water the garden. It was a low-maintenance garden. It had beautiful cherry tomatoes, lettuce, zucchini, green peppers, arugula, *Melissa ojfficinalis* (lemon balm), peppermint, and eggplant. My landlord was so proud of the garden that he brought all the guys in the neighborhood over to see it.

I GRADUATED FROM the midwifery program in July 1991 and became a certified nurse midwife. As I looked for jobs, I was pleasantly surprised to find the red carpet being laid out before me wherever I applied. I had been an excellent student. I finally decided to take a job with Miriam, my good friend, at Beth Israel Hospital in downtown Manhattan. The director there had told her she could hire whomever she wanted, and I was her first choice

When I got there, it was clear that they were not as progressive as Columbia Presbyterian in terms of clinical protocols. For example, babies who were delivered with any degree of meconium, the dark greenish feces that have collected in the intestines of an unborn baby and are occasionally released in labor into the amniotic fluid, were sent directly to the neonatal intensive care unit for 48 hours of postpartum observation.

Treatment of meconium has changed over the years. Until recently, every baby who was born with any degree of meconium had its vocal cords examined at birth. Now we know that it is not even necessary to suction meconium out of the nose and throat of the baby while the head is on the perineum (which used to be routine).

The move to Beth Israel concerned me. I felt the institution might not be as up-to-speed on new research as I would have preferred and, therefore, might not be as open-minded. I was worried about going backward in terms of unnecessary intervention.

THE FLIP-FLOPPING OF obstetrical absolutes is a disturbing trend for me. There is something suspicious about "truths" that change every few years, especially regarding a physiological process that has not changed much since the beginning of time. This kind of thing automatically causes me to question the veracity of studies when they do appear.

I believe it started with a split that occurred many years ago, in the 17th century. The apprenticeship model that stressed the wisdom that comes with experience was asked to bow to a new model of medical education, which emphasized justifying clinical practice exclusively from conclusions of research studies. The resultant trend was that doctors-in-training applied generational truths to their clinical practice as if they were gospel and often didn't re-evaluate the underlying precepts over time. This trend continues today.

As a midwife, I have come to have great respect for common-sense wisdom and experience. In my 16 years as a certified nurse midwife, I have tested my own hypotheses of how to avoid unnecessary intervention. I have disproved many of the hypothetical assumptions I was taught in school, hospitals, and birthing centers. Here are just a few of the myths that have been dispelled for me:

- Women whose water breaks before labor begins are more likely to have their babies negatively affected by infection, if the mothers are allowed to go into labor in their own time.

- Big babies are more likely to experience damage during the birth process.

- Meconium during labor always signifies a pending dangerous scenario in terms of fetal distress.

Many, many other so-called truths have been debunked for me in my own practice as well.

Nothing is more upsetting to pregnant women than living in a state of confusion. Pregnant women are constantly looking for direction. Unfortunately, their quest usually brings them to consume their "truths" from the latest books on the subject. Obviously, not all information received in books is useless, but the rulebook should not change as new authorities come forward.

The entire pregnant population is in a neurotic state, confused about what to do and eat and whether or not they can or should exercise. This sends them in search of "experts" possessing temporary truths that do nothing to render them confident in their pregnancies. And it fosters a continual dependence on these very same experts.

MY MOM'S GENERATION delivered breeches vaginally. My own birth is an example of that. In my mother's day, women were permitted to gain only 20 pounds in pregnancy, not 40 like they are now. Women drank and smoked with abandon, but now, not even a drop of alcohol or a puff of smoke is considered okay. In the 1980s, women hospitalized during preterm labor were regularly placed on 100 percent alcohol intravenously, but when now-revered midwife Ina May Gaskin suggests a shot of vodka for the same reason, she is regarded with suspicion. One generation is told not to lift anything heavy and to rest on the couch; the next is told to maintain a steady regimen of yoga, running, and swimming. Who keeps defining these trends?

A lot of women, including some of my patients, often wonder if they are doing harm to their babies because of what the experts are telling them. Many times women have come to me wanting to deliver at home because the birthing center they had consulted had a weight gain cutoff. Why? Because it is "known" that high maternal weight gain correlates with high estimated fetal weight, which is a risk factor for shoulder dystocia. But I have seen otherwise. One woman who gave birth at home because she was told that if she gained 50 pounds she wouldn't be allowed to deliver at the birthing center had a baby who weighed only 7.5 pounds.

I know that the amount of weight a woman gains is not directly proportional to the size of the baby. I have seen women gain 60 pounds and give birth to 5.5-pound babies and other women gain 15 pounds and give birth to 8-pounders. Why can't this truth be factored into nutritional counseling? Why are so many obstetricians still using weight gain to keep their pregnant patients in line?

Rather than using weight gain as a measure, midwives devote quite a bit of time to discussing nutritional guidelines that women can use to inform their eating during pregnancy. I think it is sometimes easier for some doctors, instead of taking the time to go over a patient's nutritional needs, to feel their responsibility is fulfilled if a patient takes her prenatal vitamins. They rarely explain that women have different nutritional needs at different points in their pregnancies.

For example, it might be helpful for women to know that nausea is normal in the beginning of pregnancy, as are all kinds of food aversions. There's a reason for it: the baby's organs are forming and this is Mother Nature's protection against introducing potentially harmful things into this very important time of organogenesis. At the end of pregnancy, women crave carbs and can't stop eating. There's a reason for this, too: this is when the baby is putting on most of its subcutaneous fat.

Anemia is also common during pregnancy. Most obstetricians will do a complete blood count (CBC) to document the hematocrit — percentage of red blood cells — and hemoglobin levels, and then prescribe various iron supplements. But rarely will they address nutritional corrective measures. I often tell my patients who are anemic to combine iron-rich foods with others that are high in vitamin C, as the acid promotes the absorption of iron.

One great remedy is to cook tomato sauce in an iron skillet. For my vegetarian and vegan patients, I recommend fermented soy products, such as tempeh and miso. I also sometimes prescribe pharmaceuticals, such as Iberet-500, an iron supplement that provides much-needed iron without causing constipation.

One of my patients, Blaise, was curiously not treated for anemia at all by her obstetrician. She decided late in her pregnancy, as she was approaching 36 weeks, to have a homebirth. During our second prenatal visit, she mentioned that she was experiencing what felt like bronchitis. The symptoms resembled what she'd experienced in her first pregnancy, when she wound up with pneumonia. She said she'd been treated with a Z-Pack, a five-day dosage of Zithromax, and asked if I'd prescribe that again to prevent pneumonia. I decided it was a wise choice.

I didn't receive Blaise's prenatal records from her doctor until she finally gave birth. But if I had, I would have had greater insight into why she might have been so susceptible to infection: she was clearly anemic. According to her records, her hematocrit level was only 29 — a normal level during pregnancy would be 34 or above. Because her hematocrit level had been so low, I prescribed what is now Iberet-500 but was then called Fero-Folic-500. I wanted to give her an extra boost after pregnancy. I wondered why her condition hadn't been addressed by her former provider.

BY SPENDING A LOT of time in hospitals, I got a real education into the psyches of the medical and nursing staffs. The ob-gyn field can be very territorial. I can't say that I'm exempt, either. I got a real feel for that in my job at Beth Israel Medical Center.

I remember one instance in which a very young Orthodox Jewish woman came to the clinic when she was far along in her pregnancy. She had been a clinic patient at a hospital in Brooklyn that didn't employ midwives in labor and delivery and had decided very late in the game that she wanted a midwife instead of a doctor. Due at any moment, she asked me if she could work with a midwife at Beth Israel. I told her that she might not be treated very warmly if she just walked in while in labor, but if she had her records, she might be subjected to less intervention. She did come in while in labor, requesting to have a midwife as her provider. Oddly enough, I happened to be working in the labor room that night.

As soon as they got her into a labor room and out of earshot, the female chief resident said, "Put blades on her," meaning "use forceps." It seemed the resident was punishing her for picking a midwife. It's comedic to think that someone with that kind of authority could be so unethically punitive. It took the mother four hours to push the baby out, and all the while, the MD wolves were howling at the door, forceps in hand. But, of course, a little passion and urgency got the baby out in time, naturally.

At one of our weekly meetings at Beth Israel, the director of midwifery schooled us on the hierarchy of care. This was before the famous scandals there, like "Dr. Zorro" signing his patients' abdomens with his initials, or a woman dying from fluid overload while having a benign ovarian tumor removed because they let a product rep run the machine during her surgery. She let us know that if several patients came in at the same time, the private practice patients should be taken first. After that, when triaging the clinic patients, we were to make sure to take the patients from the satellite clinic that served the Jewish population first, and to take the patients from the Ryan-Nena clinic in the Hispanic Loisaida area of the East Village last. I was appalled. It was bad enough that this woman could even think such things were okay, but to openly say them?

Beth Israel never felt like home. I lasted there for only six months. I was actually asked to leave, which became the only blemish on my résumé. Through a series of misunderstandings and unfounded speculation, my boss thought that I had been performing homebirths. It was considered a conflict of interest. I hadn't been performing homebirths, but there was no convincing her otherwise. So I was out of a job.

I found myself in the midst of another one of those cosmic kicks in the butt that hurts me terribly in the moment but ultimately takes me where I need to go. I suffered the loss of that job. But soon thereafter I was hired at the Maternity Center, where I had done a short residency while in midwifery school.

*

CHAPTER 7

Mother Nature's Son

I T SEEMS FITTING TO ME that before I started my own practice, I experienced my own homebirth. A midwife gains bona fides by having been there herself. While I do know wonderful midwives who have not had a baby, for me, giving birth was the ultimate rite of passage.

I had wanted a baby all my life. Maybe it's because I was my own mother's helper from a very young age and the second of five girls. I'm not entirely sure why that deeply intrinsic desire was always strong in me, but it was.

On some level, it seems as if I was prepped for not just motherhood, but single motherhood. Even though I technically belonged to an intact family for the first 16 years of my life, I think I came from a long line of metaphorically single moms, some with husbands officially in tow — if not all along, then for at least some of the time.

Ours was a matriarchal tradition started by my paternal grandmother, Adrienne Jaeger. She had taken the very courageous step of getting rid of an abusive husband back in the mid-1930s. This guy was my grandfather, although I hate to honor him with such a distinction. He was *tough*. I mean, what loving father tries to teach his young son, my dad, that the stove is hot by holding his hands up to the flame?

My grandma must have been one hell of a proud strong female if she could make the decision to leave that situation. It meant that she would have to tolerate the stigma of being a single mom, something society frowned upon in the Depression era. She obviously loved her son more than she concerned herself with what people thought. Her father, Wilhelm, took over the fatherly duties. He was mostly German but of some Hungarian descent. My grandmother returned to her maiden name, Muhlhahn, and gave it to my father as well. Matrilineal descent was particularly progressive for that time. Did I inherit a culture of matriarchy or the psychological fallout of abuse? Whatever the answer, these are the roots from which I have grown.

All of my grandmother's adult life, she worked as the office manager at a restaurant called Sid Allen's in Englewood Cliffs, New Jersey. She was a very dedicated grandmother — my only one, really. My mom's mom died in her early fifties of nephritis. I was only 5 then. I do remember her letting my sisters and me eat Cheerios with chocolate milk, but that's the entirety of my recollection. She was our *Nona,* which is Italian for grandma. Only my older sister,

Kim, and I knew her at all. And wouldn't you know, she was single, too, at least by the time she was my grandma.

Even though my father was present when I was growing up, I had a sense from the time that I was very young that raising children was the exclusive jurisdiction of the women in the family. Three of my four sisters had kids before me, and all of them either chose or fearlessly accepted single motherhood as a suitable consequence of their desire for children. Kim had decided to have a son on her own before entering into a long-term lesbian relationship. Laura, the sister directly after me, got pregnant in her senior year of high school. She and her boyfriend were very much in love and got married when she was just 18. They remained married for eight years, but when they divorced, she found herself on her own.

Naturally, by the time my turn came, I had grown comfortable with nontraditional expressions of family. Motherhood took precedence over becoming a wife or partner in a relationship, which meant that we didn't put a lot of effort into securing a marital foundation before moving on to childbearing. That might sound backward to some people, but for me — and my sisters, I think — it seemed a completely natural choice. My sisters and I have been great moms, a Muhlhahn family tradition I'm proud to revel in.

IT'S NOT AS IF I HAD never given any thought to establishing a solid relationship before becoming a mom. As a younger, dating woman, I had considered being part of a duo first.

Of course, it would be a feminist-era, egalitarian relationship. I thought I should secure a financially reliable profession to release a potential partner from the traditional obligations of breadwinner; then, we'd have equal time to enjoy the nurturing aspect of parenthood.

In fact, I recall a conversation that took place with a man I was dating in my early thirties. He was imagining how cute our babies would be. I said this would be a good time for me to have a baby because I only needed to work three days a week, which would give me more time to be a present parent.

"How about you?" I said.

"I have a business to run," he replied.

I realized then that coming to the table offering a 50/50 split in terms of money and responsibility wasn't every man's dream. It was crucial for me, though. I wanted to ensure the continuation of my work, even while choosing motherhood. Ironically, the power and security I developed somehow led me to attract, and be attracted to, men who came to the table with way less, some of whom took advantage of my foundation. I didn't always recognize that in time.

Even though I had always wanted to be a mom, when I turned 35, my desire took on an urgency heretofore absent. My clock was ticking. I realized that I hadn't quite coordinated the two aspects of life that many see as intrinsically intertwined: creating a solid, lasting love relationship and then having children. A few years before, when I was with Ronnen, the potential for a love child within that relationship had presented itself. But that was ultimately not to be. I wasn't sure that option would pass my way again.

I hate to admit it, but I know it's true that the tick-tock of my biological clock came into play. It's amazing how that inner voice suddenly progresses from a whisper to a shout. When it was at it loudest, I had a boyfriend. He had green eyes, tawny skin, and a poetic soul. His name was Geoff. We had met at Barry Harris's jazz class. He played piano. I was in the singer's class. We began a relationship, but we hadn't progressed to the point of making a lasting commitment.

I was very much in love with him. This was good, because more than wanting to secure a partner who was stable in terms of position or possessions, one of my criteria for finding a mate was that my child be born of that certain special love chemistry that Geoff and I possessed. One night, when we had been together for about a year, I said, "I love you! Make me a baby!"

At that moment, an invisible conduit opened its doors, and in flowed Liam. I felt it happen. This is why I always believe pregnant couples when they say that they knew the moment they conceived. I believe that sometimes, even the guys know.

Nothing compares to the excitement I felt when I missed a period. I had all the signs: breast tenderness and frequent urination. By Day 27, my period still hadn't arrived. My cycle was typically short, around 25 days. Sure enough, I was pregnant. My due date would be June 19, 1995, which was also my father's birthday. Considering that only about

3 percent of women actually deliver on their due dates, I didn't really expect my father and son to share a birthday. And they don't. Liam was born on June 27.

I LOVED EVERY PART OF being pregnant. At 37, I initially felt old for a first-timer, but that didn't detract from my joy or make me worried in any way. I was so ecstatically, unbelievably happy that I was having my first baby. Because I had helped so many women through their pregnancies, I thought I would know what to expect at every turn. I looked forward to everything, even the nausea. Until it actually hit at Week 5.

Fortunately, as often happens with women carrying boys, the nausea was short-lived. For three weeks, I ate lemon pops and sniffed peppermint teabags for minor relief. I also had the "bionic nose" pregnant women are famous for. In New York City, there are few places a pregnant woman can walk without feeling an aversion to breathing. It also led to some socially awkward situations. One time, I insisted on sending a steak back in a favorite French restaurant in the East Village, even though none of the friends I was with could smell anything wrong with it.

During my pregnancy, I continued to study singing and to perform. My two passions, jazz and midwifery, were battling for attention and dominance, though. Pregnancy, with its assorted bodily distortions, threatened to redefine and possibly even forever alter my jazz-singing aspirations. I had to face that things were changing. My pregnancy made singing difficult. It affected my lung capacity and my pitch. Simultaneously, I learned that for me to keep my voice in great working order, I should remove some polyps from my vocal chords, which involved surgery. I decided that elective surgery wasn't for me. Any lingering thoughts of pursuing singing as a career were put to rest. I went back to reveling in my pregnancy. But pregnant or not, I knew that music would always be a source of lyrical and rhythmic joy.

I can't say that Geoff shared my excitement and enthusiasm about the pregnancy. As soon as he realized the consequences of his actions, he freaked out. Granted, he was only 28 at the time. His attitude may have been a natural one for him, as it can be for some men. I've seen even very committed husbands have this reaction. But it was a complete bummer for me. It seemed like the biggest rejection imaginable. I should say in his defense that despite his panic, he never pressured me to terminate the pregnancy. Thank god!

I was slow to spread my news at the Maternity Center. During my second month of pregnancy, I'd munch red raspberry tea–infused ice cubes as a way to distract myself from my severe nausea, never revealing my big secret. It's hard to imagine, though, that the other midwives and the birth assistants were blind to it. Once I came clean, everyone at work celebrated my pregnancy. I loved the staff there, and they took special care of me during my pregnancy, often extending my one-hour lunch periods to three hours of naptime in the third trimester. I felt so blessed and coddled.

MY PATIENTS AND I BONDED in a new way, as well. Now I was one of them. They knew that I was experiencing along with them the whole enchilada of discomforts, concerns, and magical feelings they were having. They also knew that I was moving toward that uncontrollable, unknown event called labor that they were anticipating as well. Being pregnant made taking care of other pregnant women even more fulfilling than it had already been.

In addition to working at the birthing center, I was moonlighting at Planned Parenthood while I was pregnant. It was great — I loved being a pro-choice woman and presenting my choice, while not judging others. I remember counseling one patient who was in her forties. Although her relationship was solid and her partner was comfortable with the prospect of parenthood, she wasn't sure that she wanted to be pregnant. I felt it imperative to go over with her some of the statistics relating to fertility rates for women in their early forties, as I thought she might regret not keeping this pregnancy. She decided to keep the baby, and I felt good about that counseling job.

I had many other rewarding experiences there. I helped a young Irish immigrant find the courage to speak out about having been raped and press charges against the man who got her pregnant and burned her legs with a cigarette. He was a cop, and he'd warned her there would be more trouble if she reported him. I cried during that visit. I was horrified that he had bullied her into not coming forward. Two years later, I received a card from her. In it she told me I had given her the courage to prosecute, and that I was her angel.

I HELD OFF REVEALING the news of my pregnancy to my family and friends. I didn't want to tell anyone until I had at least passed the first trimester, which made sense in terms of allowing the baby to declare its viability. The first three months can be like a trial. And since I wanted to do an amniocentesis, I figured I'd just wait until the results were in, in case there was a problem.

I chose to have the amnio in part because of my age, but also because one of my younger sisters had a daughter with a chromosomal syndrome, most likely trisomy 18, a fatal condition in which the baby has three chromosome 18s. She had given birth to fraternal twins, a boy and a girl. The boy was fine and is now a healthy teenager; his sister only lived three months postpartum, poor thing.

My sister had done some genetic testing and was told that she had been a carrier of this particular disorder that only affected girls. When I got pregnant, I was somehow instinctively certain that my baby was a boy, but I didn't want to rely exclusively on instinct and sweat out the genetic possibilities over the next nine months. An amnio would rule out all chromosomal anomalies, including Down syndrome, also known as trisomy 21, which is much more common than the trisomy my sister's daughter had.

When I went for the amnio, Geoff was having serious second thoughts about his new fate. Instead of going to get the test with Geoff, I asked Miriam, my midwife and friend, to go with me. She had offered to be my hand-holder. The poor obstetrician — whom Miriam and I both knew from having worked at Beth Israel with him — incorrectly assumed that we were a lesbian couple. He did his best to be politically correct. It was quite funny from our point of view, so we let the mystery stand.

Eight days after the test, Sylvie, my former preceptor at the Maternity Center and a good friend who was now working with the amnio guys at Beth Israel, called with the results. She read them to me so nicely over the phone, I will never forget it. First, of course she let me know the baby was normal. Then she asked me if I wanted to know the baby's sex. Before I could even answer, she said, "You know, don't you?" I said, "Yeah, it's a boy." And she confirmed. I had been right all along.

And then it hit me. *Whoa.* I was one of five girls. As a grown woman, I was still trying to figure out how to value and be valued by the men in my life. Now I was going to have a *boy?* For the first time in my pregnancy, I was nervous.

I called my sister Kim in Denmark, hoping she could shed some light on my prospects. Kim had read her son, Jonas, all the right gender equality-themed books. Still, at the tender age of two, as he heard a plane flying by, the first word that escaped Jonas's mouth was *"flumeskeen,"* or "airplane" in Danish. What is it about boys and big engines — planes, trucks, trains? This one example tipped me off to the fact that nurture had little advantage over nature in taming those raw boy instincts. I wondered how I would relate to this boy inside me who was completely unknown to me in so many ways.

Kim was completely reassuring. She reminded me how big of a role hormones can play in maternal adaptation. She said not to worry and promised me that I would love my baby, regardless of gender, personality, or looks, from the minute it was born, thanks to maternal hormones — although I don't think she put it so scientifically.

I have to say, Kim was right. On Day 3 postpartum, I bonded deeply with my newborn son. This is the day that hormonal changes bring both tears and breast milk, the day when I don't want my patients to have any responsibility except to be home with their babies for exactly this reason. Besotted with tears, I professed eternal love for him and I told him that I had been waiting for him my entire life.

Having a boy is wonderful for me in ways I never expected. Twelve years into Liam's life, he and I are very close and very much each other's best friends. We have so much fun together, whether we're body surfing in the ocean in Costa Rica or dancing together (Liam takes ballroom dancing classes!) or watching *Family Guy* reruns. He keeps the tomboy in me alive. And I am determined to help him grow up to be a good man who appreciates and is respectful of good women.

THE AMNIO WAS MY ONLY antepartum screening. I passed on all the others, including the more popular ones, such as sonograms. I had made the decision to be pregnant without a guarantee of perfection. After being a midwife for a while, as I had been at that point, a very sober perspective develops. No test or measure of normalcy can guarantee, or even diagnose, everything. I knew that I could be carrying a perfectly normal kid chromosomally speaking, yet he could still come out with just one leg. Like every pregnant woman, I must admit, I entertained a few fantastical fears. I jokingly called my baby "peg-leg" in an attempt to conquer my fear of the unknown.

I also knew that even if the baby seemed normal on all the tests, I could go into preterm labor, or have chorioamnionitis, and deliver the baby at 20 weeks. There were a whole host of other risks and potential complications, things I had seen in more than 15 years of observing pregnancies and attending births. So I knew better than to seek assurances in those tests, knowing that those assurances would be tenuous — or even moot. I just had to bite the bullet. There would be no guarantees. I actually found it kind of liberating.

WHILE I ENJOYED BEING pregnant immensely and looked forward to becoming a mom, I knew I had to deal with the reality of having a partner who was uncertain about fatherhood. I kept bumping up against that fact, and it was the one factor that kept unsettling me and the otherwise perfect picture of my life. Sometimes I would wonder if other women's husbands or boyfriends were more completely on board than Geoff was. But then, when I'd get a closer look at some of their relationships, I realized they weren't all perfect, either.

At the same time that I was pregnant, one of my fellow nurse-midwives became pregnant as well. She and I had our baby shower together. It was fun to have a colleague to share my pregnancy with. Her husband was a psychologist. One might assume that a guy in his profession would be more sensitive to his wife's feelings. So I was really surprised to hear from her privately that throughout her pregnancy, he just kept expressing his concern that she wouldn't lose weight after she gave birth. It's not as if she gained a lot of weight or anything. She looked completely fine! But I know she didn't feel attractive to her partner.

I loved my pregnant body. In fact, when I went on vacation to Puerto Rico while pregnant, I wore my bikini and felt utterly regal. I had fun with my clothes. Everything I bought was secondhand. I frequented the Goodwill and the Salvation Army, where I got my towels for the birth. I got my diaper covers at St. George's thrift shop, which used to be right across from the Friends School on East 16th Street, not far from the Stuyvesant Town apartment I was living in then.

Wearing a midriff-revealing top in the hot weather turned out to be quite an interesting sociological experiment. I collected a combination of comments and looks of plain shock about my "illicit" presentation, mostly from other women. Some gay Brazilian men I encountered, though, told me how beautiful I was and how much it reminded them of the way pregnant Brazilian women carried their bellies with pride. Why should I have hidden? I was proud and in a blissful state. I felt as though I was accomplishing a mission of great importance, which incited a certain euphoria in me. It seemed as if I would never be depressed again.

I felt beautiful and sexy, inside and out. It bugged the shit out of me that my friend's husband couldn't celebrate her new, temporary shape to help her feel like I did. During my pregnancy, I had an unusual experience related to therapy. I had signed up for a dream workshop run by a Jungian therapist. I was very excited about that, since pregnancy is usually a fertile time for dreams; it certainly was for me. The format of the course was that we were all supposed to write down our dreams on paper and then throw them into a basket. The therapist would choose a few and read them aloud. Then he'd lead the group in analyzing and discussing the dreams.

After a few rounds, I realized that my dream was never picked. I asked him why it hadn't been, and he replied, "Because you're pregnant." I wondered, *What the hell was that supposed to mean?* Was he afraid he'd say something that would upset me? Pregnancy can really freak some people out, even some seasoned mental health professionals.

Even though I was a knowledgeable birthing professional, I went through all the childbirth preparation classes parents typically go through. I spent most of the time in the classes witnessing (and lamenting) how the often-misguided pregnant women would buy into illusory, often elitist escape routes, such as thinking that the practice of yoga, for example would ensure them an easy delivery.

The trend in this country is for people to think they can maintain control over all things and to imagine all sorts of causal relationships that don't necessarily exist. While yoga might make someone feel better generally, I'll put my money on genetics playing a larger role in labor length than whether or not yoga is practiced. So if a woman's mom had a fast first labor, she is more likely to do so. And the more of a control freak she is, the longer the labor she will probably have.

Birth professional or not, on some levels, I was still a true first-time mom. I worked full-time at the Maternity Center until my due date. There I was on that very day, delivering a baby, kneeling down with the mother, my belly dragging on the floor. I suppose it was a good idea for me to work right up until that date since distraction was essential; I wasn't yet in labor, and it looked as though the big event might never happen. I called my mother and told her I was okay with just staying pregnant forever; I could return the baby clothes she'd sent.

My sister Kim had arranged to come in from Denmark for the birth. I couldn't wait for her arrival. I picked her up at JFK Airport on the evening of June 24. At 1 AM, all of a sudden, there was clear fluid leaking from my vagina. I just looked at it as if I had never seen it before. Geoff, in bed beside me, said, "I think that must be your water breaking." Miriam suggested I go to bed and get some sleep, which

I did without a fight. So many primips have to be talked down from the jittery excitement of labor beginning to the more therapeutic state of sleep. But I knew the routine, so I went to bed.

The next morning, I called Miriam to tell her that contractions had begun. It was happening. Or at least I thought it was.

Everybody came over to be with Geoff and me at our apartment: Miriam; her assistant, Jan, who had offered doula and filming services as a gift; my sister Kim; and Melissa, my very good childhood friend. Melissa also lived in Stuyvesant Town with her husband, Bill, and daughter, Mikayla. "Stuy Town," as those in the neighborhood tend to call it, was a great place to reside, especially during my pregnancy. It's a sprawling apartment complex just north of the East Village. It has its own roads and grass and trees. It was built by Met Life as affordable housing for World War II veterans, and it stayed affordable until its apartments were recently converted to full-market value. Toward the back was a fountain where I would walk and relax and breathe the fresh air in my first trimester and then again during labor.

In a grudging attempt to bring on labor, I walked with my little entourage around what is fondly referred to as the Oval, a Stuy Town path, while some of my neighbors cheered me on. I don't know how Miriam kept a straight face. She knew, as my posse knew, that it was ridiculously early on in the labor process and that I wouldn't deliver for at least a couple of days.

If I had delivered at the birthing center where I had worked prior to starting my own practice, I might have had a cesarean section because I was not in labor within 24 hours of my water breaking. Protocol would have required that no matter how the baby was doing, I be given Pitocin — a synthetic form of the natural hormone oxytocin that's used to induce or augment labor — to bring about contractions and to reduce the infinitesimal risk of infection. I would have been given several vaginal exams that would, ironically, have put me at greater risk of infection, which might have led to the administration of antibiotics.

But that wasn't an option, as far as I was concerned. At least not yet. I was at home in labor and everything was fine.

The night before, I had noticed a very strange phenomenon. My feet began to swell. They looked like two bulbous, oversized yams, misshapen to the point of being unrecognizable. To humor me, my sister went out and picked up a massive tuber that bore a close resemblance to one of my feet. I had never seen that before, nor have I seen it since in any pregnant woman I have ever cared for. I still don't now what that was about. In any case, it passed, and then I was onto bigger hurdles.

That night, I went to sleep in my own bed. First, though, Miriam took my temperature to make sure I wasn't developing an infection and she declared it normal. She was back and forth to visit me for the next couple of days, since nothing was happening. Finally, at 56 hours after rupture of membranes, she suggested that I take castor oil. Castor oil, a laxative, is often used to induce labor. No one knows exactly how it does that; maybe delivery is a by-product of emptying the bowels. I acquiesced without a struggle. I swallowed a bottle of Neoloid, a product that is unfortunately no longer available in the United States. It was great because the castor oil was emulsified and had a peppermint flavor that cut the lousy taste and smell, which probably reduced the tendency to puke it right back up.

I was familiar with castor oil. In fact, at the birthing center where I was working, we used Neoloid. When it didn't work, patients ended up with Pitocin inductions in the hospital. I so preferred to do this at home, knowing full well the advantages of having the freedom to wander around on my own and sit wherever, even in the bathtub if I wanted to. Six hours after taking the castor oil, the serious three- to five-minute contractions began.

My sister Kim turned out to be my best doula. She worked with me on the breathing. That helped to bring the fear that came with the pain down to a level I could handle. The fact that she was my sister and she had been through this helped me tremendously. I could use her experience as a barometer for my own. With Kim by my side, I was able to look past my pain and the temporary but acute resentment over my current condition, and think, *She did this and survived. I just might, as well.*

THINGS SEEMED DIRE TO ME during the labor; I look back now with humor and compassion. I was in quite a state. I wanted my mother, even though I had never planned for her to be at my labor. She lived in Ithaca, New York, a four-hour drive away, and wasn't about to swoop in for the rescue.

I remember hiding in the bathtub. Poor Miriam came in to encourage me to walk and get things moving, but I stubbornly refused. I wanted out. I had put some Stadol, an opiate painkiller, in the fridge for just this occasion.

"How about that Stadol, Miriam?" I asked. But I knew better. I've never known Miriam to use pain meds in labor. At that moment, the idea of a C-section seemed pretty good, or at least an epidural. I promised not to be one of those women whining at an International Cesarean Awareness Network meeting about my unnecessary C-section. No, mine would be justified. *There was just too much pain!*

Miriam tried to talk to me. "Car, you're nine centimeters dilated. No one at the hospital is going to give you an epidural at this point."

I said, "Yes they will. I'm a health care professional."

It is important to note that I had specifically told Miriam during my pregnancy that if I had a cesarean, I would be really depressed. It was very important to me to give birth vaginally if at all possible. Of course, the staff at Beth Israel would have had a good laugh if Miriam and I, who had both left Beth Israel under unfavorable circumstances, showed up for a homebirth transfer. *My own homebirth transfer.*

I thank Miriam now for saving me from having a C-section, but in the moment, I wasn't exactly the picture of gratitude. She had blocked all of my escape routes, and the rest of the crew was banding with her. I remember perceiving the palpable empathetic doubts felt by my true friends over my sorry state. But they were avowedly under Miriam's influence and didn't dare do anything to rescue me. If only she weren't the one in charge.

I got in the tub and just stared at the faucet. I don't know how long I looked at that focal point, but at some point, it finally occurred to me: I couldn't get the section, and the pain of pushing was probably just as bad as the pain of staying right where I was, with the feeling of a rock covered in glass shards lodged in my ass. This was the epiphany I needed. I got out of the tub, walked out of the bathroom and down the hall, and got fully behind the idea of second-stage labor and the miserable pushing it required.

The pushing took one hour and fifteen minutes. That's not bad compared with how long some primips' second stages can last. I gave up any notions of being dainty and just gave it all I had, while my face took on the fierce, anguished look of Aztec birth goddesses. Goodbye, vanity!

Still, it seemed, nothing was happening. I was sure that Liam wasn't even moving down. Miriam did an exam on the couch. Feeling her fingers was a reassuring thing, a connection to some help. She said, "Cara, I can see the baby's head."

Well, I wasn't going to be falsely encouraged. And I told her so: "That's because you're holding my vagina apart," I snapped.

Poor Miriam. I only learned recently that I had made her cry during my labor and birth. It makes me sad to think about that. How many friendships can survive that kind of intense experience? But now we're more than friends; we're two midwives bonded for life.

I eventually realized I just needed to do this and that it was something that only I could do, even with my loving cheerleading squad around me. Looking to anyone for help was just a distraction keeping me from the ultimate relief of pushing that kid out. Finally, everything changed. Melissa and Kim had shifted their attention to my vagina. They were looking directly at it, which was a sign of good news. Geoff was holding me up as I pushed while squatting. His gentle murmurings encouraging me to push were like nectar from the gods.

Everyone was back on my side. They really were of great help to me. I knew we were almost there. Then there was that unfamiliar sensation of burning I had heard so much about, a feeling that often comes when the baby's head begins to crown. I made an otherworldly noise, something akin to the screeching of a hyena possibly heard on the National Geographic channel. Progress! No one could take it away from me now! I was on the other side of that huge divide.

Liam came out angled slightly clockwise, in left occipital anterior (LOA) position with his head facing downward. He then rotated 90 degrees to left occipital transverse (LOT) to face my right thigh, which is fairly typical, and Miriam gently guided him into my arms. I wish I could say that I was overcome with bliss, overjoyed with the birth of my son. I'd love to paint a picture in which my face gracefully morphed from laboring Aztec birth goddess to beatific saint as I embraced my perfect child. I'd get there a few days later.

But the truth is, right after birth, I was too completely traumatized by the pain and the whole ordeal. In fact, I think I might have called Liam a little bastard. He cried for 20 minutes after the birth, and I remember thinking in my posttraumatic stress disorder frame of mind, *He's probably realizing that his mother is a bitch.* Liam was only calmed by Geoff's rhythmic, reassuring lifting and bouncing. That was the beginning of an extremely bonded daddy-and-son relationship.

FOR A MIDWIFE, I was a bit clueless about the demands of the postpartum period. All primips are clueless to a certain extent, but I was in the business, so it seems even more ridiculous that I thought I might take piano lessons during my three-month maternity leave. *Ha!*

My immediate postpartum experience was complicated by a rash that developed around my waist and up and down my legs. This is very uncommon. As a child, I had always been a very allergic person, to everything from bees to poison ivy, and every childhood illness from chicken pox to the mumps hit me hard in terms of itchiness. I had learned at a young age to be disciplined about not scratching during the ravages of rashes. But this postpartum rash was serious. It drove me to use corticosteroids, which didn't even work. I finally ended up using a combination of ice and a homeopathic product called Sssting Stop. I knew that if the itching became impossible to tolerate, I could take antihistamines. But they're notorious for drying up the body, which doesn't bode well for breast-feeding.

My sister Kim stayed to help me for two weeks. I'm thankful, because I hadn't yet achieved veteran status in terms of newborn knowledge. She, on the other hand, could interpret each of my baby's cries accurately. She knew when he was hungry, gassy, and just plain bored. I wondered if I would ever be that expert. I cried at the airport when Kim left. I believe that was a first in terms of tearful departures for us. I had needed her so much and I wasn't used to needing many people.

Geoff played a huge part in Liam's care. Sleepless and catatonic, we struggled along in the throes of new parenthood with all of its unmastered tasks. I had sustained a perineal tear during Liam's birth that I hadn't wanted repaired, and now it smarted. There were days when I sat on the living room floor in a modified sitz bath, soaking my sore bottom, while simultaneously applying black tea bags warmed in the microwave to each nipple to prevent cracking and soothe the raw pain from my new foray into breast-feeding. That took some adjusting to.

Whenever my delicious baby cried and needed to feed, I would have to put music on and ice my nipples to tolerate latch-on and sometimes sip on a glass of wine or indulge in some ibuprofen. That lasted nine days. I knew I would get through it and never considered stopping nursing, even with my new understanding of how challenging it was and why so many women don't get past that first stage if they're not deeply committed. My mom had breast-fed all my sisters and me. I had witnessed her feeding my younger sisters, so I knew I would soldier on. I realized this initial pain was normal and a much smaller hurdle than the one I'd just gotten over.

I WENT BACK TO WORK at three months postpartum. It is so hard to leave a new baby! I cried all the way, even though most days Geoff would bring Liam up to see me at 10 AM, only two hours after I arrived at work. I was always grateful that I could have him safely plugged in at the breast while on breaks at the Maternity Center.

Geoff would often hang out in the neighborhood, weather permitting, so that I could feed Liam every couple of hours in the morning. Once we got the latch-on and breast-feeding thing down, Liam and I both loved it, and he didn't want it any other way. The first time Geoff tried to feed him from a bottle, he screamed and held out for my breast the whole day. We had to experiment with a few different nipples before he would accept a bottle, but we finally got him on board. Of course, he was getting pumped breast milk through the bottle; he was just rejecting the method of administration.

Geoff was handling all of the child care when I couldn't, which wasn't too often, because, fortunately, the schedule at the Maternity Center was brilliant. It was nothing like my life now, where I'm always on call and anything can happen at any time. At the Maternity Center, we did two 24-hour shifts and one 12-hour shift each week. The first half of each 24-hour shift was at the birthing center, and I was on call at home for the second half. I think that was the best schedule I've ever had in my entire life — and for a decent paycheck, too. Sometimes, if I decided to do my call on-site for whatever reason, I could bring Liam to spend the night with me.

There was just one oddity there: the director asked me not to breast-feed in the waiting room. I could never understand what that was about. A birthing center that promoted breast-feeding didn't want that very activity to be seen in the waiting room? All I can come up with is the director's own Victorian prudishness, as nothing else made sense. I found it very difficult to comply, and if I did, I felt completely disturbed about it. Ultimately, in June 1996, when Liam was a year old, I would leave the Maternity Center.

HAVING A NEW BABY can be a great distraction from disharmony in a relationship — for a while. Eventually, though, the uncomfortable realities of my relationship with Geoff became more evident. When I was pregnant and faced with his ambivalence, I think I somehow hoped that it would all change once the baby was born. But it didn't.

At Christmastime, Geoff, Liam, and I went to Denmark to visit Kim. I believe it was there that I began to plainly see how much Geoff wanted to leave the relationship. It became clear to me that we would need some serious work if we were going to stay together. I got pretty depressed because I knew I was alone in wanting to make it work.

Things went downhill after we came back, and by early summer, he had gone to Florida with some musician friends to take a new direction in his life. That was right around when Liam was turning one. Prior to quitting my job at the birthing center, Geoff had committed to watching Liam so I could start my own homebirth practice. When he left, my whole plan went up in smoke!

So, during Liam's naptimes and at night, I perused the Internet (which was brand new in 1995) for potential au pairs. Within the course of a week, I picked Karin, a 19-year-old Austrian girl. She turned out to be an angel who saved my life in so many ways. With the hiring of Karin, I had to say goodbye to my idea of using the second bedroom as my office. One night, I cried so hard thinking that my new practice might not get off the ground. I cried and cried until I was exhausted and empty. Then my resurrection idea appeared: I would have to use part of my bedroom as my office. The next day, I excitedly bought curtains to hang all around my four-poster bed. I set up the exam table, my desk, my scale, and everything else practice-related in the spacious other half of the room. After I launched my practice, sometimes patients would ask, "Is that your bed?" and I had no choice but to admit the truth: it was. But I got past that, and so did they.

Liam got plenty of attention from me and his new au pair, but I couldn't help noticing with pain that he would wander to the door once a night around 10 o'clock. I knew he was looking for his dad. I would tell this to Geoff on the phone when he called from Florida. I wasn't trying to guilt-trip him but I felt he should know his son missed him.

Geoff came back to New York in October after six months away. He said he would never leave his son again. But he was done with our relationship.

✳

CHAPTER 8

Instinct and Intellect

WHEN PEOPLE ASK ME what I do for a living, the most logical and accurate response is for me to say, "I'm a certified nurse midwife in private homebirth practice." For some reason, though, I find those words daunting. I have to take a deep breath before uttering them. Even after 12 years of practicing on my own, I am only now growing comfortable with the full weight of those words. Homebirth midwifery is a huge undertaking, filled with risks and responsibilities. Day to day, I manage it all very well, but it seems overwhelming to me when I take a step back and look at it.

I don't think it was my ambition to strike out on my own in the way that I ultimately did. When I look back at my time as a lay midwife at clinics, then studying nursing and midwifery, and finally working in hospitals and birthing centers, I realize it was just the end result of a natural progression. The decision-making process to work for myself was similar to what I went through back in my twenties when I realized that I could only learn so much in Oregon and then Texas. At the birthing center, there were limitations in both the perspective and the methodology that made it impossible for me to offer women what I consider to be the best possible care. I knew that to do the kind of work I felt good about, to be the best clinician I could be, and to offer the highest level of individualized, humanized care, there was nowhere to go but to my own private practice.

The four years I spent at the Maternity Center had rounded out my midwifery education and also confirmed for me my preference for homebirth. Birthing centers are popular now. People view them as some kind of happy medium — a little bit hospital, a little bit home. They see it as a compromise between the cold, clinical world of the hospital and the perceived lack of safety at home. Women are given their own "comfy" rooms to deliver and recover in. But they're not home. And for the most part, these centers apply clinical guidelines similar to or just slightly more progressive than those of a hospital.

My reasons for leaving the birth center had a lot to do with personal clinical excellence. For example, I felt frustrated with the way the center induced mothers so soon after their water broke. I found that most first-time moms don't go into labor right away after breaking their water. They tend to have two or three labors, and I believe that that is directly related to the mechanics of how the baby is presenting. My son was born at home 72 hours after my water broke. I received very few vaginal exams. Today, this is a great clinical issue to talk about because studies now support waiting safely for at least 72 hours. The value of *not* examining women is still barely factored into the safety equation. I guess that concept is something for future studies.

At the Maternity Center, I had been the one to suggest a period of waiting of at least 48 hours — after preparing an incredibly in-depth and well-documented review of the literature — to no avail. Nobody at the birthing centers was listening then. Now, at least they're beginning to.

IN THE YEAR THAT LIAM was born, the Maternity Center made some big changes. Those changes made it even easier for me to choose to leave, in spite of the fact that I was essentially a single mother and would lose the financial stability and security that comes with a steady job and salary.

The owners of the Maternity Center decided to sell the beautiful East 92nd Street Victorian townhouse they were in, move downtown to St. Vincent's Hospital in Greenwich Village, and change the name to the Elizabeth Seton Childbearing Center. As part of the change, the midwives were transitioning. They were trying to determine the appropriate business and legal format for their operation. Would they be working for, and salaried by, the hospital, or creating a private practice? Would the midwives be willing to have regular first-call staff and a backup second-call staff? The second-call midwives would be called to work if one of the laboring women attended by the first-call midwives was in need of a transfer to a hospital. This would permit a first-call midwife to accompany her patient to the hospital and stay with her there during labor, while a second-call midwife would come in to take care of the patients back at the Center.

Our staff had never had this sort of arrangement before. In the past, we would accompany the laboring mom to the hospital and leave her in the care of hospital staff. I wasn't too keen on the old arrangement. It had the potential to compound a mother's feelings of disappointment from the transfer with feelings of abandonment. When things did not go as planned, her midwife would suddenly leave her because there weren't enough people to hold down the fort at the birthing center.

Too often, I'd bond completely with a couple while going through all their prenatal visits and counseling and then not be on call when it was their time to deliver. It was dissatisfying for them, and it was dissatisfying for me. The last thing I want is to not be there for a mother when it's her time to deliver. Inherent in the structure of shift work is the inability to make good on the sort of commitment I consider crucial. Even though I was technically doing my job, not being on call when it was time for one of my patients to deliver made me feel as if I'd broken a promise.

Other than me, my colleague Sylvie was the only one during the restructuring discussion who expressed a willingness to do second call. It just sounded like too much work to the others. I didn't want to assume it was too much work before I actually knew. Plus, I intuitively felt it would give us a chance to come closer to an ideal in terms of continuity and individualized, intimate, humanized care. Our established system, it seemed to me, compromised women's experiences. I wanted to go for the option that would complement a birthing woman's ultimate feelings of success. I knew I would be happier with that option.

I wasn't afraid of more work. I have always had a penchant for working hard, long hours. Maybe I just have the constitution for it. My mom intimated that I was a workhorse even at the tender age of two, when I would help her with the laundry.

Not surprisingly, second call was voted down by the staff. That was just one reason I was reluctant to make the shift to Elizabeth Seton with the rest of the midwives. The next hurdle for me was dealing with the fact that we'd be moving to a Catholic hospital, which meant we would not be able to counsel women regarding contraception. I took a brief glance back at the early 1900s and decided I wasn't about to assist the Catholic Church in undoing all that birth control activist Margaret Sanger and those who came after her had achieved.

The last straw for me came to light in a business meeting. A consultant was brought in to lead our transition. One of the topics of discussion was how to market to clients who wanted epidurals so the Center could attract business and stay profitable. That just about sealed it. They were talking about labor support that contradicted the very ideals the birthing center was founded upon, just to bring in more business. I began to wonder what ideological satisfaction I might get out of such a working situation. I don't want to suggest that I'm unwilling to serve women who choose epidurals. That's not what it was about. Rather, I wasn't willing to change the fundamental underpinnings of clinical practice for monetary reasons. In my life, I've never done things that way. I'm no sell-out.

I knew I had to move on from this job, despite being a single mom with a son to support. I had the pride and integrity to live and work according to my beliefs. I trusted that support would be there as it always has been, whenever it has become clear to me which direction I need to move in. I knew that things would work out if I did the right thing.

After learning a tremendous amount on the job at the Center, I was able to leave knowing that I could handle what I imagined to be the most risky birthing situations. I had recently handled my first case of shoulder dystocia and my first baby resuscitation successfully. I decided to forge a solo path. Some of the positive results of that choice became evident only years later. Sylvie and I were the only ones who voted for second call, and she and I are the ones doing private practice now.

OF COURSE, STARTING A private practice in my Stuy Town apartment was an even shakier proposition now that Geoff had gone. With one bedroom occupied by Karin, the au pair, and the other bedroom pulling double duty as an examination room and sleeping quarters for Liam and me, I experienced my share of lapses in confidence. It was hard to feel totally legit. I had never run my own business before and had no example of entrepreneurship in my family to fall back on. It was hard not to be concerned with making enough money to cover my expenses and take care of my kid.

In spite of feeling like a neophyte, I also felt the winds of change lifting me and easing my transition. As I was leaving the Maternity Center, the new director, Maureen Cory, let me know that any equipment I wanted to take along with me would be available for a small donation. So, for a mere $100, I walked away with an obstetrical exam table, an adult scale, a baby scale, a microscope, a lot of books, some chairs, a desk, a mercury blood pressure cuff, and birthing instruments that I still have and use today. I am forever grateful for and feel very attached to these things — which I still use in my practice — because of their beneficent origins.

I was pretty much ready to go, except that I needed a backup doctor. State law requires homebirth midwives to have at least one doctor with whom they have a signed formal agreement to practice. Miriam, who helped me in so many ways to start my own practice, asked her backup doctor, Dr. John Maggio, a doctor of osteopathy, if he would cover me. He said all I had to do was call his receptionist, Eileen, to set up an appointment to meet with him about it. That seemed simple enough. I called. And then I called again. The receptionist kept stalling by not getting back to me and refusing to let me make an appointment. Frustrated and eager to get started, I figured out a way to get around Eileen: I booked a gynecology appointment with Dr. Maggio.

I arrived at the office, and Eileen gave me a cup to pee in and a gown to change into. She didn't realize I was the midwife who'd been calling and calling. I was supposed to change into a gown and wait in the examination room. *Uh-oh.* I didn't know how far I could go with my deception. Feeling like a complete liar, I stayed in my clothes. Besides, it might be really awkward to ask him for coverage if I was nearly naked.

Dr. Maggio came into the room, and I instantly blurted out an apology for not changing and explained the real purpose of my visit. I suppose he could have thrown me out of the office, but he didn't. I was grateful for that. I finally understood why Eileen had tried to protect him. He was the kind of good guy who just couldn't say no. Lucky for me! Over the years, backup doctors have come and gone. I have appreciated them all, but I will never forget that it was Dr. Maggio who made it possible for me to get started.

I now had a legal homebirth practice, but I had very few patients. No one had heard of me yet. My first patients came by way of referrals from Miriam and Sylvie, previous patients of mine at the Maternity Center, and midwives at Elizabeth Seton. These days, without ever having advertised, I have more patients referred to me than I can take on. I see four to six patients a day and deliver up to ten babies a month. When I started, I delivered only two or three a month and I remember how excited I was when the first ones came my way.

It was showtime. My education and training as a clinical nurse midwife had prepared me for the work, but it hadn't prepared me for the business side of things. Judging from what colleagues tell me, I'm not the first midwife for whom business was not a strong suit. Many of us are like artists in that way. I'm sure there are some who are more business-oriented, but I don't know many of them. There was so much I didn't know about running a business, including billing and keeping books.

Once again, Miriam came to the rescue. She had been in practice for three years already when I started. She showed me the basics of billing. It made sense, she explained, to bill patients only once, after everything was over. One code, one bill. Easy. I could handle that. I was able to do it on my own for a couple of years, while my census was low. But when I started to have more patients, I hired Ann Marie, an aspiring midwife who had been working at the Elizabeth Seton Childbearing Center, to help me in that area. She came to my apartment and did my small amount of billing. We had a lot of fun working together. Back then, I kept all of my appointments in a Filofax. I have since graduated to a PalmPilot.

Eventually, Ann Marie needed to move on, since she was going to midwifery school. I asked one of my former patients, whose husband was a pretty famous fashion photographer, whether they knew of someone who could be a good personal/administrative assistant for me. They sent me the name of their former assistant, Hitomi. I hired her right away.

Like so many other people who just meet her, I initially got Hitomi's name wrong. I called her Satomi. I remember the day I met her in front of my Stuy Town apartment. She was an adorable, sweet soul, possessing so much inner — and outer — beauty. Hitomi had been born at home on Long Island back in the late 1970s. Her mom had been quite a forward-thinking and progressive woman for her day. Naturally, Hitomi was quite excited about being part of the homebirth movement.

Hitomi brought sweetness and care to my life. I had no idea I needed so much help. As with most self-starters, I had to learn to delegate. For the first time, I was someone's boss, and I needed to get used to that. That took quite a bit of psychological homework, which I continued to do with my Jungian therapist, Priscilla. Being a super-competent person and having always relied exclusively on myself, for better or for worse, it was hard for me to trust that someone else could do a job that I had previously done successfully.

But I knew that I had to share the power to move into the future. Businesswise, I wasn't a complete disaster, although I was pretty close. As a practitioner, I always had savvy and dedication. I could always love and care for my patients with devotion because I am archetypically configured as a service person. But I don't think I could have moved forward to my current place without Hitomi's administrative leadership.

Hitomi and I developed a devoted and loving work relationship. She always had my back, which helped me in many ways to find and know my value. Our relationship also helped Hitomi find a voice of her own. And if it differed from mine, I never wanted or needed to squelch it to maintain my position.

My favorite moments with Hitomi were the ones in which she would say, "I've made an executive decision." For someone like me, who has always been in charge, it was a foreign but welcome change to experience another person coming to the table with great ideas and the ability to make important, informed choices. It was nice to have someone with whom to share the burden. What's more, Hitomi, with her keen business acumen and strong sense of what's appropriate, chipped away at the rough edges of my structure and presentation, much like a sculptor, polishing and refining it until the shiny undersurface emerged.

Shortly after Hitomi started working for me, we moved to a new three-bedroom duplex that I was lucky enough to get in the East Village. I was one of very few who qualified for these new subsidized apartments. Miraculously, through a community lottery, I had been offered the option to buy a townhouse sight unseen. Once again, it felt as if my struggles were always balanced out by my lucky star. This new apartment provided not only more living space for Liam, the au pair, and me, but it also provided a separate room for my practice.

We moved on October 28, 2001. I won't forget the day, because Hitomi was off work, and I was at a labor in Williamsburg, Brooklyn. I had to have the moving company first pick up the keys from me. Then they had to proceed, unassisted and unsupervised, to move everything from my Stuy Town apartment to the new house. Some things broke, and I never found my video camera after that.

After the birth, I remember it was late and quite cold. I didn't have enough cash on me to pay the movers. The head mover and I drove around the East Village from one ATM to the next. They each had almost reached their daily limits, so I had to visit several before I collected enough money to pay him. But I was moving up in the world. Any apartment moves I'd made in the past were with the help of friends. This time, I could afford to pay professionals.

IT WAS SO KEY FOR ME, emotionally, to have a rock like Hitomi behind me at the office. A private homebirth practice is quite an undertaking. The level of responsibility is high. It calls for me to reserve my mental faculties for all sorts of clinical strategies and challenges, not to mention unexpected events. Having someone so reassuring and reliable on top of the scheduling, the accounting, and the phone calls frees me up to be the clinician and advocate my patients need me to be.

There was so much more to working independently than I could have possibly anticipated. I was glad that I was finally the one in charge of the big judgment calls. I had grown tired of doctors calling the shots and not giving women enough information or time to make important birthing decisions. I was happy to have left behind institutional protocol. My new role was not without some serious stress, though. The part that I had never imagined was the solitude I would feel with every decision I made. I was soon faced with challenges that would both test me and help me build my confidence. I can speak with authority now, but it was built on careful trial and error and on having had to take the responsibility and the heat for each and every decision that was made.

I remember one situation early on that helped me find the fine line between protecting patients from legitimate danger and protecting them from excessive interventions at a hospital. A couple came to me. He was Greek, she was American, and they were both very warm. The husband was put off by the way he and his wife were treated by doctors. He didn't like that the doctors didn't explain things in a humane way or that they seemed to practice defensive medicine. The couple was looking for a homebirth with a midwife, he explained, because they wanted to feel comfortable and at ease in the birthing process and go through it in their own surroundings.

Of course, he was preaching to the choir. I was really happy to meet them and liked the idea of helping them with their birth. But there was a problem. The wife had been experiencing hypertension during her pregnancy. So during our consultation, I asked if I could take her blood pressure.

It was 160/90, which is very high. I measured her fundus — the top of her pregnant uterus — and she measured a bit small. I was concerned. I became conflicted. While I wanted to provide the couple with that more humane care they so longed for, a homebirth is not the best setting for a mother with hypertension.

I called Miriam, who gave me a very good piece of advice. She said, "If her blood pressure is 160/90 now, what's it going to be like in labor?" I needed to hear those words, because my work at the birthing center had never placed me in the position of making the *final* judgment call.

I told the couple that as much as I wanted to help them, it would be better for them to go back to their regular ob-gyn and probably deliver in the hospital. I later learned that they subsequently sought homebirth from two other midwives. By the time they got to the third one, the baby was dead.

Professionally, I felt relieved on two counts. First, I had made the right call. Second, part of making that call was knowing that I was in over my head and having the humility to reach out and consult someone with more experience. That's partly how a sense of judgment is developed — with the help of more experienced mentors.

Midwifery is very serious stuff. When I retire, the part that I will most look forward to giving away is the stress of living with the burden of maintaining safety. It is a very unique kind of psychological stress, and I won't miss it one bit.

IT'S HARD TURNING AWAY patients, but sometimes I have to. It's not just that my practice has grown so much and there's only one of me. There's another factor: homebirth isn't for everyone. Sometimes there are mitigating factors that are medical, as with the mother who had hypertension. Other times, it's a matter of emotions and personality. Many women think they want a homebirth but don't realize that they are too nervous and fearful. They've been seduced by the idea of homebirth, but they're not up to the challenge emotionally, and many times they don't even know it.

It can be tough to turn away parents. It's a difficult message to deliver. I recently said to one woman, "Listen, I wouldn't be doing you any favors by cajoling you into doing a homebirth. If you are really nervous about it all the way up to the birth, you're going to wind up in the hospital."

I went over the risks and statistics associated with births at home versus those occurring in the hospital, and then said, "If you don't reach a certain comfort level, I'm going to recommend you go with a birthing center or hospital birth." Then I implored her to revisit her own personal fears and make sure that in her gut she felt safe at home.

More often than not, though, the women who come to me are committed to having a natural homebirth with a midwife. They might be a little bit nervous, too, but not insurmountably so. They usually know someone else who's had a homebirth, or they've had one themselves before. Referrals come to me from past patients, from hospital midwives like

Sylvie, and from supportive doctors like Dr. Jacques Moritz and Dr. Eden Fromberg.

Some of my moms have already had their pregnancies confirmed by a doctor, but some have not. What many women don't realize is that an over-the-counter pregnancy test is usually reliable enough. If a woman misses her period, goes to the pharmacy, pees on a stick, and the results come up positive, she can be pretty sure she's pregnant without going to get a blood test at the doctor's office — and paying for a visit.

I do the first consultation and examination in my home office. All subsequent appointments — there are about ten of them over the course of the pregnancy — are done at the pregnant mother's home, with the exception of a postnatal exam six weeks after delivery. I feel strongly about conducting prenatal visits in the family's home. This is where delivery is going to take place. But more than that, it presupposes an egalitarian relationship, while allowing for a genuine sense of trust to develop between the whole family and me. That goes a long way toward helping the mother be at ease through her pregnancy and delivery.

The stage is now set, as much as it can be for birth at home.

※

CHAPTER 9

A Day in the Life

HERE'S WHAT A TYPICAL home visit is like. Marina, a patient who lives in Howard Beach, Queens, is in her first trimester with her fifth child. Marina has been looking forward to our visit. It is not our first time working together; I've already delivered three of her four kids, and I'm about to deliver another one for her. It is easy to park here. I just pull right up in front of the house, although here the neighbors definitely watch carefully. They want to make sure I meet their approval.

I knock on the door of her basement apartment. When I enter, Marina is teaching the kids at the kitchen table. She homeschools them. I get to see all the girls. How they have grown since the last time I've seen them — it's been over a year, maybe even two! But I saw Marina more recently, as she had assisted at the birth of a woman from her church. I love seeing her, and she is just as happy to see me.

Marina loves being pregnant, and I enjoy her glow. Before we officially start the prenatal visit, though, her daughters treat me to a little show-and-tell. There's a princess costume, a book, and a review of the play they put on last week. I am their special guest. The girls scramble for the floor to give all of the important news to me. I sit on the floor with them. I'm not really a chair person. I have to greet the cat, too, although he's definitely not taking to my presence as well as the girls are.

We planned this particular visit for a time when Valnn, Marina's husband, could be present. He is a public school teacher and talks proudly about informing his middle school science students of his wife's pregnancy and their plans for a homebirth. It's like a big reunion. Aurora, their oldest daughter, and Liam are the same age. Aurora is starting to bloom. Marina tells me she behaves like Hitler with lipstick. We commiserate kindly about the challenges of raising a tween.

After I take out her chart — I don't need to repeat her history because I have it all down on paper from her previous pregnancies — we go straight to calculating the due date. We drag out the calendars to be sure about the first day of her last menstrual period. The last thing we want is any lack of certainty that might make it appear, down the line, as if Marina is overdue when she's not. We go over their schedules closely. Was Valnn away at any point, and if so, when did he return? We figure after four kids together, this one is not the milkman's. We can joke like that because we have a mutual trust. And the trust between a midwife and her expectant family is given and taken seriously and with honor.

After we catch up on whatever details I need to know to estimate the due date accurately, the black "doctor bag" comes out. All the kids know it. They have all had the chance to dig into it and remove the tools: a fetoscope, a stethoscope, a blood pressure cuff, and a measuring tape. The toddlers drag these things around while I have Marina lie down on the couch. Since she is under 20 weeks, we don't need to use my measuring tape, which is housed in a whimsical plastic pig. Pull it out by its curlicue tail; roll it back up by pressing on its nose. I like using fun tools because they appeal to kids who are about to have new siblings.

When its time to listen to the heartbeat, we try with the fetoscope. Even though books and teachers will say that the fetal heartbeat can't be heard with the fetoscope before 20 weeks, I have heard it as early as 15. Marina would prefer not to expose the baby to an unnecessary ultrasound.

We can hear it! It is very faint, so we turn down the radio, and the kids have to stay very, very still, waiting their turn to listen. It's thrilling to witness their excitement. Some of them hear it; some do not. Marina and Valnn do. It's interesting: Even with all of the proof — a missed period, a positive pregnancy test, nausea, fatigue — so many women remain uncertain that the pregnancy is a reality until the first time they hear the heartbeat.

If we couldn't hear the heartbeat with the fetoscope, we might have heard it on the Doppler, which I bring to each visit in case. The Doppler is a handheld six-inch sonar device with a wand that can be placed on the abdomen and used for monitoring. Marina's blood pressure is normal, as it has been with each pregnancy. I write down my data. We look at our calendars to consider times for our next visit, and discuss what, if anything, she may need to prepare for.

I have been at Marina's about an hour. I explain to the kids that I will be coming back soon. As I drive away, I wave goodbye to one of the girls, Maya, from the window of her grandma's apartment upstairs. I had to wait for her to install herself in the window before driving away. We wave furiously and all is well. I've got about 30 minutes to get to my next appointment.

THAT'S USUALLY HOW IT GOES: 45 minutes to an hour with each patient and 30 minutes travel time in between. It allows me to see four to six patients a day, which is very manageable. It also allows me to spend quality time with them in the comfort of their own environments. Of course, that's a much lower census than in most busy doctor's offices. They may see 20 or more patients in a day for mere minutes each. The patients usually have to wait a half hour or so for the doctor to come in while they're cold, dressed in nothing but a hospital gown, and seated uncomfortably on a table.

I'm not getting rich doing this. I certainly don't bring in doctor's wages. But that was never the point. Offering women honesty, choices, comfort, and personalized, high-quality care satisfies my soul in a way being a doctor never would have.

The satisfaction I get from midwifery makes it worth the high degree of dedication and sacrifice. My work takes a lot out of me. But I like the adventure that midwifery brings to my life. I like having to drop everything to answer to a higher calling, the ruggedness of hard work, and the idea that when nature calls, there is no choice but to answer.

Don't get me wrong — I'm not always found in a perfect state of grace when the pager goes off and I have to jump. Sometimes, it's hard to rally, like when a primip calls when she is in what I know are the very early stages of labor. I don't always want to get in the car and go all the way to the Bronx to see her, spend three hours with her, and then go home because she's only one centimeter dilated. I know I'm going to lose my parking space and maybe not find one where she is. In those moments, I call on something I learned from my mother: *Do the action and the feeling will follow.* When I lack the willingness to do a particular good deed, I just do the deed, and the feeling comes afterward. It's one of the few Catholic-school lessons my mother truly valued, and it works. Once I'm in the car and on my way there, it hits me: this first-time mom, who has no idea what to expect, is going to feel so much better with me there to suss out her situation and tell her what to expect next. My crankiness melts away.

It's hard to describe the satisfaction I get from my work in a way that does it justice. I find it absolutely thrilling both to facilitate and witness the triumph a mother experiences when she delivers her child naturally in the support and comfort of her home environment. Those feelings are what make me okay with doing crazy things like spending whole days killing time in people's neighborhoods or sleeping in my car overnight, around the corner from them, so that I'll be near enough to a patient when she is ready to deliver. I've slept in my car several times after I've had an evening phone conversation with a mom in labor, usually a multip, because things often turn the corner very quickly from the beginning of active labor to delivery. Rather than put pressure on her to know when to call next, I head her way a little early so that I don't have to feel rushed if she calls me and things are going quickly.

I can't sleep in my bed at home knowing that I might be needed, so sleeping in the car reduces my anxiety and allows me to rest at least a little. There have been times when my radar was off, and I slept in the car only to go right back home in the morning. I then had to come back the following day for the birth. I never let the parents know that I am doing this because I am trying to avoid the fishbowl effect.

If I were to go to a woman in labor's home and nothing was happening, I might actually get in the way. Many women, with their midwife on hand, would feel pressured to make something happen and guilty for calling too early. By getting in my car ahead of the game and hanging out there until the next call, I'm taking the pressure off the mom, while also making sure I don't miss the birth if she figures out very late in the game that it's time to call the midwife. Sometimes people look completely shocked at the speed of my transit time, but they are always grateful.

These overnights have given birth to a little fantasy about going on *Pimp My Ride,* the MTV reality show where they customize cars in cool ways. I would ask for a backseat that pulls out partway into a really comfortable bed. There would need to be some kind of electrically controlled shade system and a refrigerator that runs off the car battery to keep things cold throughout the night. A satellite traffic alert system would be great, as would a heating system that doesn't cause emissions. And, of course, a sign that lets me park wherever I need to, whenever I need to. And I'll take a siren, too, thank you very much.

I REMEMBER SLEEPING in my car one time in Queens around Christmastime. A mom there was having her second baby. She called and said she was just beginning to have contractions. They were regular but still only seven minutes apart. She said she'd call if there was any change. Looking at my clock, I figured that change she was waiting for might come right around morning rush hour, and I didn't want to feel anxious about driving on the Long Island Expressway in that kind of traffic. So I went to her neighborhood, parked, and slept in the car.

By 10 the next morning, to my surprise, I hadn't heard from her. I called and asked if I could just come and check on her. She said things had slowed down, but she okayed my visit. When I got there, the tree was up, and her sister-in-law, who'd had a homebirth many years ago, was there. After I arrived, I noticed that the mom would wander into the other room quietly about every five minutes. It's not unusual for laboring moms to need to get away from everyone. But I started to get suspicious that something more was going on, and I asked if I could check her. She was fully dilated and had the baby about 30 minutes later. It turned out the only reason she didn't have an urge to push was because her water hadn't broken. When it finally did, things happened *fast*.

Because she was a multip, I could very easily have missed that birth if I hadn't been just around the corner. It's such an easy — and unfortunate — mistake to make. The mom says everything's okay, because it is. But if that water breaks, the baby is out in three minutes. Times like that, I ask that the woman lie down while I'm in transit to try to slow things down.

Beth, a woman having her third baby, lived on the Upper West Side. Getting from the Lower East Side, where I am, to the Upper West Side is one of the worst commutes in all of Manhattan. Beth called me at 9 PM and said that she didn't need me yet, although she had been contracting mildly all day. There was bloody show. She just wanted to give me a heads-up. I quickly got in the car and on my way. I was with Jenna, a dear friend, an East Village compatriot, and my favorite doula, whom Beth had hired. As we were crossing Central Park, Beth paged me. Since I was driving, Jenna called her right back. I listened carefully to Jenna's side of the conversation, gauging the action by her responses. Beth said something, and Jenna inferred that Beth's water had broken.

In her reassuring way, Jenna said, "That's good."

Then I said out loud, "No it's not!" Pedal to the metal, we made it to Beth's 11 minutes before the birth.

Another time, I parked myself for the day on Staten Island for a mom whose last birth I'd missed by three minutes — one of only two births I have ever missed. She called in the morning to say her water had broken, and I jumped in the car. I wasn't going to miss this one, too. I went to her home to check on the baby. After I had evaluated the baby as stable and set up a system for relaying information about baby movement and temperatures, instead of going back to my home office, I went to a nearby park to read. I decided to kill the day on Staten Island.

We spoke several times on the phone, but nothing was happening. My patient had no idea where I was when we spoke. She went for a walk in the park with her family. Still, nothing. Until about 4 o'clock in the afternoon. The mom went back home to relax, and her husband took their three daughters to the Shaolin Temple for their regular lessons. Her mother, visiting from Italy for the special event, went up to nap on the third floor of their home. With no one around, my patient went into labor. She had the baby about 30 minutes after she called me with contractions. I was glad I was close enough to get there in time.

Not all homebirth moms are multips with quick second, third — or seventh — labors. Many times, I spend at least 24 hours at a family's house while a primip is in labor. I might need to monitor a mom or a baby particularly closely. In those situations, I need to be on-site. Depending upon how well I know the family, there's the potential for awkward moments. Sometimes I just need to crash and get a couple of hours of shut-eye, or I'm just starving and need to eat whatever they've got in the fridge.

Sometimes, when I say, "Okay, I'm going to take a nap," and get ready to lie down somewhere in their apartment, I'll get a concerned look from the dad or the grandmother. But it's what I've got to do. I've learned not to be bashful about that. I am able to stay awake for long periods of time and still function, but I've also developed discipline. I know I have to take care of my needs so that I'm able to be at the top of my game when the crucial moments roll around.

I try to get the other people who are there in support of the mother to take care of themselves, too. People watching a birth have a natural tendency to feel guilty about resting or eating when the person they love is going through labor. They're so conflicted, because they feel as if they have to be completely selfless and suffer along with her. But I tell them that to help her, they need to maintain their own energy levels. They often seem relieved to be given permission for things as basic as sleeping and eating.

WHEN I'M OUT AT A patient's apartment for hours and hours, or overnight, I'm not the only one sacrificing. My kid is, too. His whole life, Liam has had to deal with having a single mom who's on call 24/7. Since I began, though, I have always known the importance of making time for Liam.

The first year I opened my practice, I asked Miriam if she could cover for me during August, just for patients' questions or emergency visits. I don't schedule appointments or take patients who will deliver in August. For the past two years, I've added February as a second month off.

Miriam said, "Cara, you can't take a month off in your first year of practice!"

"Watch me!" I replied. I yearned for the downtime of motherhood: cooking, reading, swimming, and just hanging out with my kid. And, I needed to decompress from the demands of pager-dominated living. In recent years, Liam and I have spent my two months off together in Costa Rica. It helps to be too far away to be called into action. During my time in New York, there are no weekends away or off, just the ritual of Sunday night salsa dancing to my favorite Afro-Cuban band Nu Guajiro. And even then, I'm still on call, so I have to be careful with the libations.

Liam deserves a medal. Granted, his father is also very much involved in raising him and often covers for me when I'm not around. And for Liam's first five years, I always had an au pair living with us, which made it easier to handle overnight deliveries and other situations in which I wasn't available for him. But I know it has been hard for Liam. He has always known that that beeper can go off at any time, and then he has to be second priority.

Liam's a real trouper, though, and he has been from an early age. I think I might have passed down to him the soul of a person in service, something I believe I inherited from my mother, who taught young men in prison for many years after my parents divorced.

There was one particular experience when Liam was three that inspires me so much. I got paged late at night, and I said, "Honey, I'm gonna have to go help a mom push a baby out." This is how I always said it because I often feel it's disempowering to a mother for me to say that I'm delivering her baby. No, she is.

Liam looked at me with these sad, puppy-dog eyes and said, "Oh, Mom, don't go!" But before I could even respond, he changed his expression and said, "No — you have to go."

I think he takes pride vicariously in what I do. He knows that I'm providing a service. And he knows that he's part of it because I constantly acknowledge that he makes sacrifices for me.

But it hasn't always been so easy for him to adjust, like when I haven't been there when he woke up, or for dinner, or for Christmas. When he was about four, I did miss Christmas. A woman in Larchmont, up in Westchester County, was having her second baby. She broke her water on December 23, which was before her due date. She went into labor before I had a chance to culture her for beta strep, a potentially lethal bacteria that up to 30 percent of women can carry. I had seen her a few days before, during a blizzard, when I didn't have my prenatal bag because I'd just come from a labor. I figured I'd come back the following week to culture her, but her water broke before I had a chance to return.

Now I had a bit of a clinical challenge on my hands. I had to watch her carefully to make sure the baby wasn't at risk and to put her lawyer husband at ease. So the day before Christmas, there I was, heading to Larchmont. The mother didn't go into labor right away, even though it was her second baby. I gave her castor oil, and still nothing. In the meantime, I was giving her an antibiotic every four to six hours just as a precaution so that if she did have beta strep, the baby wouldn't get it.

At a certain point, I realized I wasn't going to make it home for Christmas. I hadn't even gotten Liam any presents, not to mention a tree. In my family, we had always maintained a tradition of getting a Christmas tree at the very last minute because we could get a bargain. It's a tradition I've kept up as an homage to my father.

I called Geoff and said, "Why don't you take Liam to your mom's house for Christmas?" They always had a nice Christmas celebration. He agreed, and they spent the day at Geoff's parents'.

Late on Christmas Day, the baby was born. I finally made it home on the twenty-sixth. Liam and Geoff met me at the apartment. As soon as I got to the door, Liam asked me, so innocently, "Mom, why didn't Santy Claus come?"

My eyes welled with tears and my throat constricted, but I held it together. "Well," I told him, "because I was at a birth, and so all the doors were locked and he couldn't get in."

He thought a second, and then asked, "But, Mom, don't we have a chim-uh-ney?" My heart was broken. I didn't know what more to say. At a later date, Nicole, the birth mom, wrote him a beautiful letter expressing her gratitude for Liam having been without his mom on Christmas Day.

Because of my demanding work, Liam has had many surrogate parents and families in his young life. While away from him, I have always loved and missed him deeply. I arranged my professional life in such a way as to be able to spend as much time with Liam as I could. I did prenatal visits when he was in school so that I would be done with work by the time he needed to be picked up. I always tried to create as normal a home life as possible, helping him with his homework, having dinner with him, watching his favorite shows with him. But the pager has always kept things unpredictable, so I've needed a whole backup network of babysitters.

When Liam was in pre-K, I attended a kid's birthday party where I met many moms, among them my now dear friend Elida, a soulful woman with a great heart. She was a stay-at-home mom who lived on my block, and she has a beautiful daughter who was in the same school Liam attended, The Neighborhood School. We clicked, and I proposed the job of babysitter/backup mom to her. We made a mutually acceptable financial arrangement and worked together for quite a few years while Liam was in elementary school.

If I had a labor while Liam was in school, I would call Elida. She would pick him up and take him home to her house after school. In the middle of the night, I would call and wake her, apologetically. I'd drive Liam down half a block, often handing him to her wrapped in a down comforter, and run back to my car, always in a hurry.

One time, in my haste to get to a laboring mother, I fell on my butt on the stairs with Liam in my arms. He hit his leg, and it got scratched. Poor guy.

In his half stupor, he cried out, "Why did you do that, Mom?"

And all I could say was, "It was a mistake. This is an emergency and I was moving too fast, and that's it. I can't be a nice mommy right now." I felt terrible, but I knew I just had to get out of there right then.

Liam remembers that, and I think he mostly derives pride from it. A few years later, I was walking him and his friend Luca home from school. It was just days after I had done my first neonatal resuscitation at home, and I had told Liam about it. On the walk home, a few steps ahead of the boys, I heard Liam tell his friend very proudly, "My mom saves lives."

WHEN ELIDA TIRED OF being on call for me, which anyone would have sooner or later, Carol, another fellow single mom friend, took over. She lived only about two blocks away, and Liam was friends with her son, Lateef, whom I had delivered. With the new arrangement, the kids got to enjoy occasional sleepovers and walks to school together.

I will always feel indebted to all of the people who have helped me out in this way. Even though they were all paid fairly, I know that they watched Liam and rolled with the punches of my unpredictable schedule out of the goodness of their hearts.

IT'S NOT JUST LIAM I'VE LOST precious moments with. I missed my grandmother's passing. I recently received a letter of appreciation from the mother who was in labor that day. She hadn't known that my grandma was dying as her son was being born, and why should she have? I had kept it to myself.

She was a primip, and it was a long labor. We were both tired, and so we laid down — she on the bed, breathing through her contractions, and I, on the floor, wondering how my family felt about my not showing up for my grandmother's last moments. But Nanager lived in Ohio. There was no way I could leave to be by her side while on call. Yes, I suppose I could have asked Miriam to cover me, but it's not that easy to leave a woman in her time of need.

I also nearly missed my mother's passing. It was in March of 1997, when I was 40 and my practice was young. My mother had lung cancer and was very sick. She had decided to die at home, which seems fitting to me in so many ways. I wanted to go visit her, and I made a couple of attempts. I told the two patients who were ready to go about my trip, reassuring them that I would be able to make it back from Ithaca — which is about three and a half hours from the city — in no time. I told Miriam I was going, so that if anything happened and I couldn't make it, she would be ready. But pregnant women are skittish.

The first time I attempted to make the journey, one of the two patients, who was having her seventh baby, paged me reporting the kind of contractions that could inconclusively indicate false labor or early labor. So an hour and a half north of New York City, I turned around, only to realize when I got to her house that it was just her nerves playing with her. The next time I went to see my mother, I made it all the way to Ithaca. But then, in the middle of the night, one of my patients paged me with contractions. So I drove back maniacally in about three hours — and, of course, she never went into labor, either.

By the time I did get to my mom's bedside, she was already in a coma. I had missed her last days of consciousness. I don't know if I've forgiven myself for this.

I wailed at my mother's bedside. I spoke to her because I learned in nursing school that hearing is the last sense to go. I was trying to think of what to say or do to soothe her, when I remembered that when we were kids, she used to sing "Danny Boy" to us to put us to sleep at night. So after telling her that it was okay to let go, that she had been a good person in her life, and she shouldn't be afraid, I began singing. She then exhaled for the last time. And strangely, on cue, "Danny Boy" began playing on the radio upstairs. I got chills. I hadn't even realized that it was Saint Patrick's Day. It was a very eerie yet lovely way to say goodbye.

CHAPTER 10

There's No Place Like Home

ESPITE THE DEMANDING, devotional nature of my work, I can't imagine doing anything else. There is no question in my mind that home delivery is my true calling. Over the years, I have become deeply connected to each family I've worked with, and to each woman I've helped through this transformative experience.

But I confess that the demands of midwifery in private practice have contributed to what some might consider an underdeveloped social life. I guess I enjoy investing whole-heartedly in a few pursuits and a few people, with Liam, my only child, primary among them. I think that slowly, over time, I have grown into my work and the sacrifices that are part of it. It gives my life purpose and a balance that I enjoy as I participate in helping restore what I consider to be a necessary balance of power in women's lives. There's a spiritual element, as well. It gets deeper as I go on, as I witness more and more divine grace and learn from it.

The pact I've made with my patients is a simple but sacred one that I feel compelled to honor: I will be there for them. It doesn't matter if my car dies or terrorists attack New York City. I will be there, as I was even right after the attacks of September 11, 2001, when parts of downtown Manhattan were barricaded and I had to plead my case with assorted police officers to let me drive through.

"I'm going to deliver a baby—at home!" I insisted. "She'll deliver unattended if I can't get there!"

I had to get out and show my licenses and all my birthing equipment before I was allowed to proceed, which was frustrating and cost me time. But I honored our pact: I made it.

I have chosen to work solo, rather than in a group practice or at a birthing center where my hours would be limited to specific shifts. Sure, my life would be more predictable. But I wouldn't derive the same degree of satisfaction I get from making sure I come through for my patients. When a woman chooses to work with me, she wants me to be the one who is there for her when her time comes, regardless of the day or the hour. And I want that, too. We go through nine months of prenatal visits and guidance. If I were off call when the big day arrived, I would feel like I was dropping the ball. That is completely unacceptable to me.

So far, in a dozen years, I've had conflicts only about four times. In each instance, two of my patients were in labor simultaneously. I had to send another midwife to cover until I could get there. I do feel bad when this happens, but at least the replacement is someone I trust unconditionally: my own midwife, Miriam.

Keeping my patient load fairly manageable helps. For the past 12 years, I have taken on four to eight patients a month. In the past year, however, I have expanded to ten in an effort to meet the increasing demand for homebirth. Of course, *manageable* is a relative term, impacted by how close together the deliveries turn out to be.

I find myself sometimes uttering what I call Jedi prayers: "Okay," I'll say, addressing the birth gods, "I've got six mothers due within 30 days. They won't happen one on top of the other. Right?"

AS FAR AS I'M CONCERNED, Dorothy had it right: There *is* no place like home. And like Oz, a hospital can be a strange land indeed. A homebirth is unbelievably special. It is so unlike what goes on in hospitals or even birthing centers.

Forget the gurneys and the harsh fluorescent lights, the residents and nurses buzzing around, and the mother-to-be propped very vulnerably (and counter-intuitively, I might add) on her back with her legs in stirrups. Instead, at home, in the woman's most comfortable, familiar surroundings, there's a special birthing pool filled with warm water. The woman spends a fair amount of time in tat pool, and may even deliver in it, in a position of her own choosing.

Her partner isn't just in the room, he or she is interacting with her and supporting her constantly, spooning her in bed, holding and caressing her between contractions. She might go through several days and stages of labor there, letting nature take its course, letting her pelvis make the adjustments it knows how to make, just as the baby makes its own adjustments in preparation for its descent through the birth canal.

In her own surroundings, a mother will feel more comfortable and less observed, which helps labor and delivery to progress more readily. She gets to choose and limit who is in attendance. And she gets the individualized one-on-one attention and care of her midwife. She will have a greater opportunity to seek privacy and be discreet when she feels shy, as opposed to lying on her back in lithotomy position with Lord knows how many residents and nurses staring at her vagina.

To be quite blunt, I often tell my patients that giving birth is like taking a dump or having an orgasm. Good luck achieving either of those when feeling even the least bit inhibited. We've all done either one or both of these acts at least once and know that outside factors can get in our way. Try doing them in a cold, institutional setting — on command.

Giving birth at home is an attempt to remove the institutional agenda without compromising safety. Everything is geared toward the mother's comfort, not toward freeing up beds or avoiding lawsuits. Home is a fortress of emotional refuge. We are not drastically changing the birthing mother's environment at the same time that she is experiencing one of the most revolutionary physiologic and psychological events of her life. Being in a familiar setting, surrounded by familiar things and people, will help her interact with her labor in a less directed, more personal way. She might move into certain positions and surroundings — private, quiet, dark, enclosed — that can help her psychologically let go. Supporters of homebirth often feel that this very factor has an important effect on how well labor can proceed.

Sometimes I need to step out of the way. There often comes a time, usually during the second stage of labor when the baby is descending the birth canal, when a woman's urge to push can be stalled and interrupted by my presence, even though I am the person whom she chose to have present. In those situations, and they are common, I might hang out outside of the room she is in (often the bathroom) while she is pushing and just go in a moment after to check the baby's heart rate between contractions.

ANYONE WOULD BE MOVED if they saw the way families interact around a homebirth. In a home environment, the intimacy and integrity of the family bond are strengthened because members of the family, especially the father or partner, often have pivotal roles to play. In the hospital, these key players are mostly cast aside except to hold the woman's hand and cheer her on: "Push!" At home, they can support the mother in any number of invaluable ways, from regulating the temperature of the water in the pool to preparing food or choosing her favorite music.

Siblings can be included, too, in whatever way parents wish to include them. Some parents decide to have them looked after out of the home and then bring them back right after the birth. Some siblings sleep during the labor when it happens in the middle of the night and wake up right after the baby is born. Most of us feel that if kids prepare and help with the birth, then the older sibling may experience less sibling rivalry. As one of five girls, I think I can safely say there will always be some! But in general, again and again, I have seen these contributions enhance everyone's experience.

In fact, there should be a television show called *Kids Say the Darnedest Things at Birth*. My absolute favorite kid moment involved a birth at the Maternity Center. The birthing mom had asked her own mother to stay with the kids and help them make sense of what was happening. Only the littlest one, a four-year-old boy, really needed any assistance.

The mom was in the birthing room floor on her hands and knees. There was a blue Chux pad underneath her — one of those disposable, absorbent, diaper-like pads. The boy spotted some bloody show on the pad and said, somewhat alarmed, "Look there's some blood!"

Grandma quickly piped in that bleeding was normal when moms have babies. Next, the mom was bearing down slightly, and some stool came out, which is quite normal as well, only I doubt this kid had ever watched his mom do number two on her hands and knees. So, of course, he rang the alarm about the "ca-ca."

The funniest moment of all, however, was when she broke her water and about a quart came out onto the Chux pad. When the little boy saw that, he held both his hands to his temples and exclaimed, "There's a whole bathroom in there!"

I guess he was overwhelmed by all of the physical evidence. We all wanted to laugh out loud, but we were busy doing more urgent work.

Once the baby is born at home the connection between parents and baby is not interrupted by routine procedures like early cutting of the umbilical cord, a neonatal exam, weighing, measuring, and dressing. Those things are done, but only according to the parents' agenda.

The baby won't be taken away from the mother and cleaned off before she and the little one have had a chance to bond with skin-to-skin contact, which is good for both of them, nor will it be put in a warmer in a nursery with 20 other babies — and lots of unknown airborne germs.

MUCH OF THE TIME, especially in the case of multips, home-births go pretty smoothly, making my job pretty relaxed. Those births are fairly uneventful. Labor happens, water breaks, there's some pain, there's some walking, there's some pushing. Then there's a baby, and we all celebrate. I'm not saying these births are easy for the moms, because labor is usually harder than most everyday events. But these births are not emergent, or stressful, and they happen quickly, which gives all of the players a sense of relief. Working with pregnancy and birth when there is this kind of normalcy is an ideal we cherish and strive for, while at the same time remaining humble about the possibility of unpredictable events.

It helps when mothers are in a good psychological state, treading the line between healthy optimism and rational awareness of risk. This is one of the reasons that most midwives, myself included, continue to provide free consultation when a couple is deciding how to proceed. At that consultation, we consider the risks and benefits and discuss which situations require transfer to a hospital and how they are handled. While every mother delivering at home knows there is always the possibility of a transfer, a good number of them have, during the course of their pregnancies, developed confidence in their bodies, a trust in nature, and faith in me as a facilitator. Putting the necessary time into creating this foundation makes everything easier, for them and for me.

Although homebirth is an option for almost anyone who has a normal pregnancy, I have noticed that the subgroup of women who tend to choose it often exhibit certain characteristics, such as a comfort within their own bodies, a desire to have a birth experience that is more poetic than clinical, as well as a desire to return what we both feel is some seriously missing humanity to the experience of having a baby. Often, women who choose homebirth have an ability to step into a completely new experience without being held back by excessive fear or anxiety. This ability proceeds from a view of childbirth as a natural, physiological event, not a medically mediated one.

Many midwives recognize the value of the psychological inheritance that is the result of a birthing mother's own mom having birthed successfully. Story after story reveals that daughters of women who gave birth vaginally or breast-fed bring a certain inner confidence to childbirth that is handed down from their mother's experience. Imagine the confidence of the rare gem of a woman who was actually born at home.

Sam Sifantus is one of those women. When she came to consult with me for the first time, she shared the unique story of her own birth at home. In fact, I know the midwife who attended her birth. Sam's mom, like Hitomi's, had been a progressive pioneer to have chosen such a birth at that time.

Caring for someone like Sam is like having a Dutch woman in the practice. In the Netherlands, homebirth attended by a midwife is the norm. Most pregnant moms there only see a doctor or deliver in the hospital if a delivery becomes high risk. With a patient like Sam, you can dispense with about 70 percent of the psychological demon-battling necessary with most American women who consider homebirth. No need to address all the hypothetical what-ifs so many moms bring up, claiming it's their parents who are concerned, when really their parents are a foil for their own fears.

Sam took childbirth classes with a former patient of mine who had a necessary C-section for her first baby, even though she had been scheduled for a homebirth with me. Expressing a natural, childlike curiosity, Sam asked the woman whether she could see her scar. One of their classmates refused to look at the scar because she couldn't even entertain the possibility of a C-section for herself. It probably figures that Sam, who didn't demonize the C-section possibility, had a vaginal birth, while her classmate — you guessed it — was sectioned.

Sam's birth experience was really magnificent for her. Even though it was fairly straightforward, clinically, it wasn't exactly what she had expected. She often talks about how much farther her empowerment went than what she had even been looking for. That empowerment was facilitated in part by my hanging back a bit during her labor and delivery.

After the birth, Sam came to me and said, "I thought you were going to check me more and tell me more of what to do." I didn't even tell her to push, and that gracefully allowed her to claim the power of her process as her own. Instead of being directed by me, Sam found her own ability to steer herself toward resolution. That resulted in her knowing for a fact that she found her way to the end of that journey, all by herself. By doing homebirths, we midwives attempt to offer this major golden nugget to women.

IT'S UPLIFTING EXPERIENCES like this one that help me stay my course through the more difficult aspects of my career. While it is immensely fulfilling, it hasn't always been the easiest choice. Even after I left the limiting world of hospitals and birthing centers and struck out on my own, I continued — and continue now — to face many challenges.

There are many uphill battles in this field, especially at this time, when homebirth midwives still need to fight for legitimacy. Midwives' practice seems to be constantly scrutinized as the general public has historically accepted the prevailing view purported by most doctors that we provide substandard care. Things are gradually changing for the better, but there are still so many misperceptions about who we are and what we do.

A compliment I received from one father says it all. He was fine with the idea of homebirth from the beginning. But the baby came out not breathing, and I had to do a neonatal resuscitation. It was the Fourth of July. The dad had called 911, at my request, just in case the resuscitation was not a success, which, thankfully, it was. At the end, when I was cleaning up the pool, he came up to me and complimented me on how well I'd done and on my "professional comportment." He was so incredibly relieved that I could successfully perform resuscitation when needed. I don't think he ever considered that it might be possible. At the time, I thought, *What did he expect?* But, in hindsight, I understand that patients and their partners don't necessarily get it right away that I'm medically trained.

Before meeting me, he had probably expected me to be some touchy-feely, matronly hippie who was equipped to offer little more than moral support, a hand to hold, and maybe some arcane, esoteric "woman's wisdom" — all of which is probably quite helpful. He didn't expect me to be the serious, capable clinician that I am. I'm sure that his image of a midwife was forever changed.

It's not just the general public who's confused about what a midwife actually is, but doctors are as well. And the fact that there are so many routes of entry into midwifery creates even more confusion within the field. I mean, there are CNMs (Certified Nurse Midwives), like me; CMs (Certified Midwives); and CPMs (Certified Professional Midwives), like Ina May Gaskin. The various groups of midwives have different levels of education and are standardized and regulated by different bodies, which often disagree about things like protocols for licensure. And then there are the midwives who have come to the profession through an unregulated apprenticeship. These variations make it harder to win both political gains and the trust of the expectant mothers and their families.

Among the most frustrating of our hurdles is American doctors' misconceptions, because the medical field and its governing bodies — the American College of Obstetrics and Gynecology (ACOG), for example — have such influence over public opinion. In February 2008, ACOG released a statement reiterating its opposition to homebirth — rather misguidedly, if you ask me, especially when considering that a large percent of births in Europe and Japan are done at home.

The rationale spelled out in this press release is that babies need to be monitored regularly during labor — which, *hello,* homebirth midwives do — according to standards set down by ACOG itself for intermittent monitoring. Every homebirth midwife carries a Doppler for this purpose. Every study done on the benefits of continuous versus intermittent monitoring have shown that Doppler is as effective at preventing harm and better at preventing unnecessary Cesareans than continuous fetal monitors in the hospital.

THE DATA FROM INTERMITTENT monitoring with the Doppler at home is actually what let me know that I needed to transfer Sarah, a multip in Queens, to a hospital.

Sarah planned to have her third baby at home with me after having delivered her first two in hospitals. Throughout her first trimester, she had placenta previa — a condition in which the placenta is close to or covering the cervix. If the placenta remains there, the mother won't be able to deliver vaginally, because the cervix is going to open, the mother is going to bleed, and it's going to affect the baby's oxygen supply. In the third trimester, if the placenta hasn't moved up, which it may, the recommended course of action is delivery by cesarean. A good friend of mine who is a midwife had to have a C-section because she had a complete previa, where the placenta completely covered her cervix.

My patient Sarah had been seeing a high-risk obstetrical provider who had told her, "You can't have a homebirth because you have placenta previa."

I said, "Right. But let me know if it changes."

So the doctor kept doing sonograms, and at 28 weeks, he said the uterus had grown and the placenta was now far enough away from the cervix. It had grown up and away, so he said we could proceed with the homebirth plans.

Sarah broke her water at some point around three or four in the afternoon — I know because I was playing with Liam in Tompkins Square Park after he got out of school when I got the call. She reported it was clear fluid, which is a sign that the baby's fine. She had no bleeding, and no contractions. I instructed her to let me know as soon as the contractions started, because with her third baby, things could go rather quickly.

Sarah lived near Elmhurst. The two backup hospitals nearest her were Elmhurst and St. John's, two hospitals I'd never been in. She paged me when the contractions were three minutes apart, and I headed toward Queens. As I was driving, she paged me again. I called her back.

"Cara?" she cried, "I'm pouring out blood! *What should I do?*"

I was five minutes away from her at that point. I figured it was either five minutes for me to get to her or eight minutes for EMS, and then I'd have to deal with all those lumbering dudes with misplaced agendas and no clue about homebirth.

I told her I was five minutes away, and I had an assistant, Jenna, with me. I was so happy it was Jenna; I knew I had a competent helper. During the remainder of the drive, I instructed her as to how we would proceed.

I said, "When we arrive, I'll start an IV, and while I'm doing the IV, you listen to the fetal heart rate."

We double-parked in front of Sarah's apartment building. Once we were inside, I gave Jenna the Doppler, while I quickly started her IV.

Sarah said, "You want to see the blood?" and I said, "No," because I already knew what I was dealing with. She was probably very dilated. The cervix had probably dilated up above the placenta, revealing open blood vessels, the reason for her bleeding. The only reason she was stable now was that the baby's head had come down far enough to tamponade the arteries in the placenta. Even though she was no longer hemorrhaging, Sarah had lost enough blood for me to be concerned about the baby's reserve.

The IV was in. Jenna checked the baby on the Doppler, and it was doing fine. We were in a good place, and ready for step two. I told Sarah I was going to examine her, and depending on what we found out, we were going to make a decision about how to proceed.

I knew that the baby was going to be out in five minutes once she was fully dilated, since it was her third. When I examined her, it turned out she was at ten centimeters. She was ready to push, and there was no bleeding at that point.

I said, "Sarah, we're gonna do one push and we're gonna see how the baby tolerates this push, and if the baby doesn't tolerate this push, we're going right to the hospital."

She pushed. The baby's heart rate plummeted to the 70s — we'd much prefer 120 to 160.

I said, "That's it! No more pushing!" I didn't want to be at home, since any number of risky situations could have developed from there. It was possible the baby could have been out and fine in a matter of minutes. Or Sarah could have been so oxygen-deprived that she might have fainted during the delivery. I wasn't taking any chances.

We had her out of the house and at St. John's in a matter of six minutes. Her husband, a then 200-pound Serbian chef (I've heard he's made some headway on losing a bit of that weight since then), picked her up and brought her down the stairs. Jenna drove. She's not that comfortable driving a stick and burned rubber the whole way. Meanwhile I monitored the baby's heart rate via Doppler. Everybody was stable for now.

I walked into the hospital giving report in motion, "I have a gravida three, para two," explaining as we wheeled Sarah into the delivery room that we were dealing with a possible partial previa based on her early pregnancy and clinical happenings at the labor. They saw that the IV was in, and the baby's heart rate was audibly stable on the Doppler that I was holding to Sarah's abdomen.

Sarah delivered in the hospital, and everything was fine — except they cut an episiotomy, which was just so unnecessary in a fully dilated third-time mom who wouldn't even have needed to push much. What a shame! But even with that, none of us regretted the transfer. Having a backup plan that includes a cooperative hospital is a necessary feature of a safe homebirth practice.

THE ACOG STATEMENT goes on to say, "Unless a woman is in a hospital, an accredited *freestanding* birthing center, or a birthing center within a hospital complex with physicians ready to intervene quickly if necessary, she puts herself and her baby's health and life at unnecessary risk."

Funny, because I have worked in an accredited freestanding birthing center, and the format for transfer to a hospital is the same as we follow for home: we are no more than 30 minutes away. And in a freestanding birth center, there are no physicians present and ready to intervene, either. They are in the hospital, the same one to which the homebirth midwife is potentially transferring her patient.

This statement is just one illustration of the conflict midwives have with doctors, who believe they need to have a supervisory role and should determine the legitimacy of the midwife and her actions. Other countries boast a more collegial relationship between the two professions. In the Netherlands and Denmark, midwives prevail over childbirth, and for the most part, only high-risk pregnancies and births are handled by doctors in hospitals.

In the United Kingdom, a joint statement written by the Royal College of Midwives (RCM) and the Royal College of Obstetricians and Gynaecologists (RCOG) in April 2007 states, "The Royal College of Midwives and the Royal College of Obstetricians and Gynaecologists support home-birth for women with uncomplicated pregnancies. There is no reason why homebirth should not be offered to women at low risk of complications, and it may confer considerable benefits for them and their families. There is ample evidence showing that labouring at home increases a woman's likeli-hood of a birth that is both satisfying and safe, with impli-cations for her health and that of her baby."

This statement is followed by a four-page plan of action, as the British National Health Service wishes to make the option of homebirth available to all women by the year 2009.

IT'S DIFFICULT NOT TO resent the ACOG statement's inac-curate portrayals, especially for me, a midwife who success-fully transfers patients in 6 to 20 minutes on average, even in the most emergent situations, as in the cases of Sarah and Aileen. You know Aileen already; she was the mother in Brooklyn we met in the Prologue, for whom I had to hail a cab because my car was dead.

After wending his way through rush-hour traffic on the Manhattan Bridge, our well-paid taxi driver deliv-ered Liam and me quickly and safely. We were in Dumbo, a formerly industrial area in Brooklyn that's now a chic neighborhood named for its location — Down Under the Manhattan Bridge Overpass. I got to the loft Aileen shares with her husband, John, also an illustrator, just in time.

Which was great, except then I had to figure out what to do with Liam.

I had never had to bring Liam to a birth before. I consider it inappropriate in every way imaginable for my son to be there. I apologized and explained why he was there and then stuck him in the building's hallway, where he wound up having to hang out for three hours, reading a book and doing his homework while he listened to Aileen moan in agony through the door. He was a pretty good sport, even though he knocked on the door at one point and asked to "use the can." The doula, Jenna, told him sorry, he had to wait, and sent him back out to the hallway with a plastic jug to pee in. Fortunately, I learned later, he was able to get one of Aileen's neighbors to let him do his business and then loan him a chair for his hall duty.

But I couldn't even begin to worry about my son in the hallway. From the minute I arrived, Aileen was practically crowning — meaning the baby's head was beginning to show — in the birthing pool she'd rented. I was instantly called into action, causing the rest of the world to melt away. It wasn't long before the baby came out, and then screamed — a good sign. The baby was breathing. All was well.

Except, a few minutes later, the placenta was not coming out, and the water in the birthing pool was rapidly turning dark with blood. I told Jenna we had to get Aileen out of the tub — *now*. The hot water in the tub could make her bleed more. And it would be hard to measure the blood loss if things got hairy. Which they did.

We took Aileen to the toilet, because sometimes sitting on the toilet is helpful in terms of encouraging the placenta to come out. But nothing was coming out except a lot more blood. We moved her to the bed, because if she was kept horizontal, she would be less likely to pass out. The placenta was partially attached. It had to come out, but it wasn't ready to. It had to be fully detached before the uterus could clamp down and stem the flow of blood from the arteries. I could have given her medication to help get the placenta out, but by the time I started an IV or by the time the medication got into her system, I would have lost valuable time for someone who was bleeding as heavily as she was.

I looked at Aileen and John. He was white as a ghost, standing by her head. I said, "I'm sorry I have to do this," and then stuck my gloved right hand into her uterus. Within seconds, I manually removed her placenta. Her uterus, a minute before gushing blood from her arteries because it was unable to contract and seal them off, was now hard as a rock. Whew! We were temporarily out of danger.

I put in an IV to add blood volume along with some Pitocin to keep her uterus contracted. I watched to see how she responded. If all was well, she would be coming up, feeling better. But she wasn't. The next words out of her mouth were, "I feel like I'm sinking into the bed." *Oh, god,* I thought, *here we go.*

Could there have been another source of bleeding that I hadn't stopped? There was nothing coming out vaginally. Maybe she was just behind on fluids. Her blood pressure was low, just 60 over 40, but that can take a moment to stabilize after delivery. Even if she stabilized at home, however, she was going to need a blood transfusion, at least to produce an adequate supply of breast milk.

Jenna called 911. She tried to explain the situation very calmly to the operator, who kept getting the story all wrong. John grabbed the phone from her. "Get someone over here!" he said. "My wife is going to die."

We had four of the loveliest firefighters in New York City at the loft in just ten minutes. Of course, by the time they arrived, Aileen was stable, and her blood pressure was rising. But there was no room for mistakes. It was better to have backup. The firefighters started a second IV just to replace some blood volume, but by this time her blood pressure was up to 90 over 40 or 50 — quite respectable considering what she had been through.

We all went with her, some in the ambulance, some in my car, to our backup hospital, St. Vincent's, lovingly referred to as St. Vinnie's. They might have taken us to the closest hospital, Long Island College Hospital, in Brooklyn, but since Aileen was stable, they obliged us by going the extra distance to St. Vincent's, where I'm most comfortable. Aileen received a transfusion and went home a few days later.

At the first nonurgent moment, I asked Jenna to call Geoff, Liam's dad, to have him come and get Liam. He'd been such a trouper. John later gave Liam a beautiful print of one of his illustrations as a thank you for being so patient. It is hanging on our apartment wall now. Every time I look at it, I think that of all the births I've attended, Liam had to be present, and stuck in a hallway, during the scariest one.

＊

CHAPTER 11

The C.Y.A. Factor

D ESPITE ALL ITS ADVANTAGES, homebirth remains a controversial subject within the medical community. Interestingly, though, most of the doctors who rail against homebirth *have never even attended one.* They make their determinations about the work of homebirth midwives without taking the time to study what we do. I, on the other hand, make my determinations about what they do based on having worked alongside doctors in hospitals.

My decision to facilitate homebirths came about partly because of my passion for it. The other part came from my frustration with the defensive medicine I witnessed in the hospitals and birthing centers where I worked. I watched as women were subjected to unnecessary interventions because their bodies were not meeting institutional protocol. A woman's water would break, and if she was not in active labor within 24 hours, she often underwent procedures to help her body speed up. These procedures can bring about negative consequences. For instance, examining her every two hours ups her chance of infection. And inducing her ups her chance of a cesarean section. My frustration with this kind of cover-your-ass, or C.Y.A., medicine, as they call it in the hospital, has grown over the years.

From experiences like those that happen most often in hospital births, a woman doesn't learn that her body is an amazing vessel of creation that can do things she never dreamed. This feeling, that I exist to defend, is an intangible that is very difficult to study and often lost to articulation. Instead, in hospital births, all too often a woman learns that her body *can't* do these things, and she is left with feelings of inadequacy.

So it's not only my job to help get the baby out; I am contracted, emotionally and spiritually, to help my patients courageously stick to their instinctual imperatives, to answer to that nagging higher calling that tells them this is what they were meant to do. This same calling makes it possible for me to rally and do my best clinical work even after I've been up for days, driving around from one birth to another, and maybe even getting ticketed because I had no choice but to double-park.

My patients deserve this kind of devotion from me. Each has made a difficult choice to do something that seems second nature to them and to me — to deliver their babies naturally, in the warmth, comfort, and safety of their own homes, surrounded by their partners and other loved ones — and they need my support.

I say this is a difficult choice because in our culture, many still perceive this practice as radical. These mothers find themselves fighting against pressure to give birth the "normal" way — in a hospital, where the risks of unnecessary intervention are higher and the experience is much less empowering and satisfying for the woman and her family — just to follow their deepest evolutionary instincts. And they have to do this in an environment of negative and false information.

In most hospitals, there's a nearly one-in-three chance that they will deliver by cesarean section — an overused surgical procedure that should be a last resort but has instead become mainstream. This is due to narrower definitions of "normal" birth and the fact that it saves doctors time and reduces risk of malpractice litigation. In a hospital, both baby and mother are exposed to more harmful germs and are more susceptible to infection. And with so much potential for contagion from so many people, the overuse of antibiotics and sanitization can even have negative consequences on the health of a newborn.

That's right: home is definitely safer in terms of exposure to germs! The mother's body has already dealt with the germs that inhabit her home. In *Good Germs, Bad Germs: Health and Survival in a Bacterial World,* author Jessica Snyder Sachs states, "Children absorb the good bacteria they need to have populating their own digestive tract from birth on. A Caesarian birth for example, results in a baby who is not exposed to the bacteria found in the mother's perineal area, which raises the risk of developing autoimmune problems like asthma and Type 1 diabetes." People in our culture have sanitization issues that they would like to think have a scientific basis but are, instead, purely aesthetic in nature. After the theatrical release of *The Business of Being Born,* a documentary about the homebirth process in which I appear, the director, Abby Epstein, got an email from a woman who was going to be showing the film and wanted to know what to tell the audience about why, horror of horrors, I wore gloves in some deliveries and not in others. I had to keep my cool while explaining that not wearing gloves puts *me* at risk, not the mom. The beauty of my situation is that I know each woman's infectious disease profile and, therefore, don't have to adhere to rote prevention strategies. I know my patients. Without question, I wore gloves when an HIV-positive mom in my care gave birth at home.

WHY DO SO MANY WOMEN sign up for the disempowerment and added risks that come with hospital birth? Before nursing school, when I was doing my premed work at Lehman College, I took an individual tutorial called The Sociology of Medicine. Much of what I learned there has been confirmed for me in my experience. Women are affected by a paternalism inherent in the doctor-patient relationship that facilitates their own disempowerment, and they feel too intimidated to even ask questions. A woman in an ob-gyn's office feels she needs to cooperate even though her instincts might be telling her to disagree, or question, because this person is going to deliver her baby. Her life and her baby's life will eventually be in the doctor's hands.

This results in the insidious process of turning one's own instincts and intuitions over to the advice of the experts, even and especially when it contradicts a woman's intuition. Many women make this unfortunate and unnecessary mistake. They choose a doctor they hear is "good" and then turn off their own voice, replacing it with "the voice of reason" — that of the expert. This process is facilitated even more by the hormonal state of pregnancy, which creates an unusual psychological vulnerability in the pregnant woman. By the time labor begins, the hierarchical power relationship has been conveniently laid down. It's almost impossible at this late stage for a woman to take back the power.

Labor begins with a trip to triage. After she leaves triage, where she has been evaluated by way of a vaginal examination by the resident on call and admitted into labor, a birthing mother is ushered into her private room. And what is smack in the middle? The bed! Hospital culture puts a woman in bed, attached to the continuous electronic monitor, and the suggestion of any alternative positions — like squatting or standing by the side of the bed — by doctors is just pretense. Of course, once the mom is in the bed, she rarely gets up again. And often, if she inquires about getting up, she gets heretical looks, which have the desired effect. Those looks warn, "Don't rock the boat." The next procedure is to get a "strip," which is a readout from the monitor so as to evaluate how the baby is faring.

It can be hard for women to stay on a natural course in a hospital, because so many interventions are offered so quickly and with unchallenged authority. In labor, one of the first introductions a mom makes after admission is to the anesthesia department's representative. The so-called Candyman comes in to make each laboring woman aware of her pain relief options before she is even ready to think about it.

Introducing an epidural when the mother is two centimeters dilated, when she knows there's a lot further to go and is just discovering how painful contractions can be, sets a picture in her mind of how things will eventually proceed. It becomes not a matter of if, but when, she will get the epidural. I have a good friend, an ob-gyn, who told me that she had to tell the anesthesia department that she didn't want them welcoming her patients without first speaking to her, as she, too, disagreed with this unifocal approach to labor support. This ob-gyn friend had her children at the Maternity Center where I worked before doing homebirth.

In a typical labor and delivery unit, the option to work with gravity is often thwarted way too soon by introducing epidurals, which can only be done with women in bed. Often after an epidural, Pitocin augmentation is introduced. Once on Pitocin and an epidural, the woman has to stay in bed, hooked up to continuous fetal and blood pressure monitoring. And that puts her on the slippery slope which way too often leads to unnecessary delivery by cesarean section.

I don't think even 1 percent of the women I assist at home give birth on a bed or even in a reclining position. And that's not as a result of my doing. Most of my moms naturally choose some form of forward-leaning, hands-and-knees, or standing position that a woman's body naturally finds her way into when not directed.

WHILE MANY WOMEN FIND it easier to cope with the pain of labor when they can find their way into positions that feel natural to them, in all honesty, many harbor the desire to have the option of pain relief readily available. I, who gave birth at home and had a lot of difficulty tolerating labor pain myself, completely understand a woman's desire for pain relief.

I've seen the most confident multips cave even momentarily. Mindy, a mom who was having her seventh baby at the Maternity Center when I worked, was in serious pain during the most intense phases of her labor. She got right in my face and grabbed me by the shoulders and said, "Cara, I want an epidural. I trust you." She had this maniacal look on her face that came from a desperation I knew all too well.

I said, "Mindy, I can't put an epidural in. I'm sorry, but we need an anesthesiologist for that."

Upon hearing these cruel words, she flung herself across the bed and said, "Fine then! Shoot me!" She proceeded to climb off the bed seconds later and squat over the floor. Out came her baby. I caught the baby bare-handed, as there was no time for gloves. And, like that, the pain was gone. Delivering does that.

I was glad Mindy was ultimately led back to a more natural experience. Judging by the fact that she had her eighth, ninth, tenth, and eleventh babies at home with me, I'd say she was ultimately glad, too.

Imagine this scenario in a typical labor and delivery unit, where the nurses are watching the monitors, conveniently, from the desk. How are they going to monitor Mindy's baby at the same time they're watching the other two patients each nurse has for the day? If Mindy's baby doesn't have a recorded fetal heart rate tracing, what would happen if her child wasn't okay? There would be no medical evidence to fall back on to prove that the providers' actions were defensible.

THE RATIONALE FOR THESE interventions isn't to enhance a mother's experience and well-being; rather, they are practiced as defensive medicine, based on the medical profession's fears with an eye to protect against liability. I have worked within that framework, and it was not satisfying.

Since I graduated from midwifery school in 1991, I have cut one episiotomy in more than 700 deliveries, and I knew immediately afterward that that episiotomy had not been necessary. That baby weighed 10 pounds, 2 ounces. But since then, I have helped out many even bigger babies — weighing 10, 11, even 12-plus pounds — whose shoulders needed assistance during delivery, and I did it with no injury, no episiotomy, and often, with no tearing. I have the Gaskin maneuver, an on-all-fours delivery technique developed by well-known CPM Ina May Gaskin, to thank for that. We midwives have some nifty tricks for delivering large and oddly positioned babies that doctors would be wise to learn.

Why did I cut that one episiotomy? Because the maneuvers I learned in midwifery school to dislodge a shoulder dystocia involved cutting an episiotomy. That's because the standard of care for obstetrics is determined by physicians. So I was taught to perform that standard of care so that if I were sued, I could say I had done everything I was supposed to do. I had thought that safety was the bottom line, not liability.

All medical practitioners trained in this country, including nurse-midwives, are trained to ensure safety in potentially risky situations while simultaneously minimizing the risk of litigation in the event of a bad outcome. These two themes are always presented together, enmeshed like Siamese twins. Preventing a malpractice suit becomes integrated into every clinical judgment call. The reason why doctors place so much emphasis on minimizing risk and liability is that they have come to see themselves as ultimately responsible for every element of every outcome. This simply isn't true. We are all only players in a complex chain of events.

For example, if a doctor doesn't insist that a mom who is 35 or over have an amniocentesis, that doctor may feel he is playing Russian roulette, since the incidence of things like Down syndrome starts a geometric progression at this age. At age 35, the chances are about 1 in 750 that mothers will have a baby with Down syndrome. Just five years later, at age 40, the chances are one in 1. If the mother's baby turns out to have Down syndrome and testing was not done, it is not the doctor's fault! It is no one's fault! The doctor wasn't tinkering with the egg and sperm when they combined.

All I know is, after I performed that one episiotomy, I determined that I would never again, just to cover my ass, let the defensive medicine aspects of my training goad me into doing unnecessary procedures that I would later regret and consider a violation. That realization was the beginning of 14 years of deprogramming myself from my defensive medicine indoctrination.

DESPITE BEING EDUCATED and constrained by this defensive-medicine think, some physicians still manage to support women in making empowering choices. Some doctors have taken the time to understand what homebirth is about and what midwives do, and they are very supportive of us and our patients. I have been fortunate to find some with whom I can work, and I am grateful for them and all their referrals to my practice. I work regularly with a perinatologist, a cardiologist, a hematologist, a holistic gynecologist, and assorted ob-gyns, pediatricians, and psychologists. When we work in tandem, supporting one another, great things can happen.

And hospitals aren't all bad. We couldn't do without them in cases of emergency. They have lots of intelligent doctors and machines and equipment and medications on hand that are great to have at your disposal when things are abnormal or become dangerous. They're just not great places for normal birth.

Here's an example of an effective collaboration between doctors and a midwife. Sabine, a German-born patient of mine, had her first baby with Dr. Jacques Moritz, one of my ob-gyn colleagues. Everything went fine. Dr. Moritz sent her my way when he knew that she was seeking a homebirth for her second child.

Sabine's second pregnancy went beautifully. The baby grew normally in the third trimester. At the 32-week point, the head should begin to present, so the doctor or midwife checks to see that it's doing so. Sabine's baby's head was always what we call oblique, which means that instead of being directly in the pelvis, right over the pubic bone, it was a bit off to the side.

Toward the end of a woman's pregnancy, the prenatal visits come closer together. Each time I came to see Sabine, I saw that her baby's head was moving slowly from oblique to transverse. At each visit I gently coaxed it back into the center. This happened without duress; I checked the baby's heartbeat to see if it minded being repositioned, and it didn't. From about the 37th week of a woman's pregnancy until delivery, I see her even more frequently — about once a week. During that time with Sabine, I noticed that the baby's head was moving slowly up toward the fundus, or the top of the uterus. It seemed as though the baby was sneaking into a breech presentation. This was especially interesting to me, because it recalled what my mother had told me about my time in utero — how the doctor would keep turning me but by the time we'd return for the next visit, I would have reverted to breech position.

I knew there had to be a reason this baby was turning the way it was. So I decided to take Sabine in for a sonogram to see where the cord was. I had a sneaking suspicion that the cord was around the neck, which is not usually a problem as it occurs in 40 percent of normal deliveries. In this case, however, I thought it might be responsible for the baby's continuous journey northward.

Sabine and I went together to my perinatologist, Dr. Franz Margono at St. Vincent's Hospital. We notified her husband, Ronnie, about what was going on, and he said he'd meet us there. Dr. Margono did the sonogram, and determined that the cord was wrapped twice around the baby's neck. He advised us to not *schwinger* the baby, using the German word for "swing," although it sounded more like *schvingeh*.

After the sonogram, Sabine, Ronnie, and I got dinner at a nearby restaurant. We explored the underlying meaning of Dr. Margono's advice for the next two hours or so. I explained the situation to them and laid out all the options. The implication of what Dr. Margono said was that I shouldn't force the baby back into a vertex presentation. *Ay, ay, ay,* I thought. If we couldn't get the baby back into a vertex presentation, then our options were quickly narrowing to a C-section, at least as far as Dr. Margono saw it. I had a feeling, though, that things weren't so bleak. My instincts told me there was a way for Sabine to fulfill her dream of a homebirth or, at the very least, a vaginal birth rather than a C-section.

So I came up with a plan. Up until our last visit, I had been gently urging the baby from oblique and transverse positions to vertex presentation without a problem, as evidenced by the Doppler fetal heart rate. Of course, I was wrestling with the part of me that saw it fit to bring Sabine in for a sonogram in the first place, because the baby's head was continuously rising in her uterus. I phoned Dr. Moritz, Sabine's former obstetrician, and asked him if he could turn the baby in the hospital, as a way of ensuring that the baby tolerated the turning. There, we would be able to watch the baby on the monitor for a while after turning. This might indicate that Sabine could be induced to get her into labor before the baby could turn back around. Then, we'd head back to their place for a homebirth.

For her part, Sabine would have been happy if I had just turned her baby once more. But I felt cautious with this new information about the cord being wrapped twice around the baby's neck and felt the heat of Dr. Margono's wagging "*no schvingeh*" finger. I was reluctant to turn the baby once more. My gut was telling me not to, and I felt compelled to listen to it. I was still optimistic about the chances for a homebirth, although Ronnie finally confessed to Sabine, "I was happy to go along with the homebirth as long as things remained low risk, but things have changed."

Dr. Moritz agreed to my plan for turning the baby in the hospital and then taking it from there at home. But the day that Sabine went in ended up being extremely busy. It was an inadvertent blessing in disguise. Sabine and Ronnie were there all day. After such a long wait, the baby was easily turned. The doctor who did it said that it was possible that the cord was actually just lying over the shoulder, not wrapped around the neck twice as it had appeared to Dr. Margono. He explained that sonography is not a perfect science.

The baby was monitored and was still doing fine many hours after turning. Dr. Moritz was supposed to pass by and stop in, but his office hours were keeping him. In the meantime, Ronnie called me to say the doctor who turned the baby was pushing for a hospital delivery.

The doctor told him, "Hey, you've played with this baby enough. Let's just get him out." That made Ronnie really anxious. He didn't want to do anything that would put the baby at risk.

I asked him if he — a professor — thought that the doctor had presented him with a well-thought-out risk/benefit analysis of the situation that made sense to him, as I had done the other night at dinner.

"No," he allowed. But he was uncertain how to proceed, due to the weight the doctor's statement carried.

I said to Ronnie, "Maybe this doctor is just opposed to homebirth." And in fact, when pressed by Ronnie, the doctor revealed his bias against it.

Sabine had no problem sticking to her guns in the face of all of these medical assessments. Ronnie was doing his best to conquer his own fears, which were being exploited by the doctor who'd turned the baby. I finally got Dr. Moritz on the phone, and we talked. He said the kid had been monitored there all day and was doing fine.

I asked him, "If Sabine and Ronnie want to go ahead with the homebirth, would you take us back in the hospital in the event that the baby experienced any distress?" The reason this had to be negotiated at that point was that I didn't feel comfortable, in the event of transfer, bringing Sabine back to St. Vincent's having *schvinged,* albeit in the hospital under surveillance for the whole day.

Dr. Moritz said, "Sure." My kind of doctor.

Ronnie and Sabine came across town to my office, where we made a plan for induction that night so the baby wouldn't have a chance to turn back around. The induction plan involved administration of castor oil. I decided to sleep at their house, Doppler-armed, so as to make everyone, including myself, comfortable with the baby's status.

I listened to the baby all night. The signs were all good. The castor oil kicked in gradually and the labor proceeded slowly over the course of the day, as some second labors do. Sabine's doula was there. Things just didn't seem to be moving, so we all made a plan to go take a walk on the roof of their building. About 15 minutes after we got up there, I had to guide everyone back down again, as Sabine's contractions became strong and steady. We got inside, and I got things ready for the birth. Within half an hour, her water broke and the baby came out.

And guess what? Dr. Margono was right. The cord was wrapped around the neck twice, but not tightly. If it had been, I could have handled it by cutting it. But I didn't need to in this case. I just gently lifted the cord over the baby's head once, then again, and he came out and breathed, well and beautifully. Sabine was on top of the world. She did it! I was thrilled, to say the least. And Ronnie was, too.

By taking things one step at a time, unhurriedly, and by incorporating all of the parents' feelings, as well as those of the experts, we reached a great conclusion not derived exclusively from contemplation of the risks. Yay! One more unnecessary cesarean avoided because of excellent clinical management and great collaboration.

BY THE WAY, I DON'T CONSIDER all C-sections to be unnecessary. In fact, I very much appreciate the availability of hospitals and surgeons who can perform them when my patients need them. By the same token, I see it as part of my job to remain supportive of the moms who choose alternatives like C-sections in their moments of truth — or who have no choice.

In certain cases, for a variety of reasons, women just cannot give birth vaginally. This accounts for my 4.5 percent C-section rate. And when it happens, I give those women the same love and encouragement I give all my other patients. I once had a client, Anushka, who wanted to deliver at home.

Her mom had gotten what she thought to be an unnecessary C-section, and she wanted to resurrect that inheritance for herself. She was a week overdue, and she called my assistant, Hitomi, to report that she was having some bloody show. Hitomi called me just to report Anushka's phone call. I thought, *Let me just call her and see how she's doing.*

When I got her on the phone, she sounded a little anxious. She had never sounded like that before. She said the baby wasn't moving. She hadn't mentioned this to Hitomi.

I said, "Then we need to do some juice," to which she responded that she'd had a lot of water. I said, "Well, we need the sugar to see if the baby moves." She told me she had just had a sherbet pop and it hadn't done anything. She added that when she pushed on the baby's foot, it didn't push back.

I told her to go to the antepartum testing unit at St. Vincent's Hospital, where Dr. Margono would do a nonstress test to see how the baby was doing. She did, and it turned out the baby was experiencing bradycardias, or low heart rate. Clearly, if this child was already having "bradies" without contractions, then Anushka wasn't going to tolerate labor without the baby incurring a dangerous lack of oxygen. I knew she needed to be sectioned right then.

Afterward, she beat herself up. She asked me, sadly, "Cara, why? Why wouldn't my body do what it was supposed to be able to do?"

I got very stern with her and said, "Anushka, you are the reason your baby is alive! It's because you were in touch with your baby and intuitive enough to know that it needed help." In fact, when we tried to thank the perinatologist — one of the most soulful doctors I know — for seeing Anushka so quickly, he said, "Thank the mother." That's why we work together.

I WISH MORE DOCTORS were as open to working with midwives as the doctors I work with. More are joining their ranks, but gradually. One of the biggest misconceptions some doctors promote is that their patients won't be safe in the hands of midwives. Meanwhile, I feel I offer my patients levels of safety that are sometimes no longer available in the formulaic, protocol-driven system of institutionalized medicine.

It begins with my clinical skills and knowledge. The cumulative effect of having worked in every possible setting where birth occurs is that I bring expertise from all of these experiences to create an ideal of empowerment, satisfaction, and safety. I talk to my patients honestly, as if they are intelligent adults, which goes a long way toward building trust and sharing responsibility. Above all, I provide my patients with a kind of individualized care that emphasizes heart, generosity, hope, devotion, patience, compassion, and attentiveness, something most doctors can't — or won't — take the time to do. What I'm trying to illustrate is that rapport is an important component of safety — as important, if not more so, than possession of an encyclopedic knowledge base.

The kind of rapport I develop with my patients has at times been lifesaving. For example, one patient, Caroline, gave birth to her first child at the Maternity Center when I was there. I was her midwife then, and she came to me for her second baby. A few weeks after the baby was born, I examined her. It is standard to do a physical examination at six weeks after delivery, where I listen to the heart and lungs, measure her blood pressure, do gynecological and breast exams, and check her thyroid. When I checked Caroline I found that her thyroid was visibly enlarged. I'm not a physician, and this diagnosis clearly fell out of my scope of practice. But I told her about it, and suggested that she see her doctor for a follow-up. As a midwife, I do recognize that I have a limited scope of practice, and when I encounter something outside of my scope, I refer patients to the appropriate medical authority.

Caroline said she would go have her thyroid checked. I didn't see her again until she came back to me pregnant with her third baby. She still had a lump on her thyroid. I said to her, "Caroline, what's going on? You've still got this lump on your thyroid. What did the doctor say?"

"Well," she said, "he took my blood levels and they all came back fine." I thought, *What?* This is where my own common-sense intuition came into play. Here she had this lump on her thyroid, and the doctor hadn't figured out what the heck it was. It wasn't likely to be a goiter from iodine deficiency — not in the United States where the diet is not poor in iodine. I called my backup doctor and asked him for the name of a good endocrinologist. At my urging, Caroline went to see him.

It turned out she had thyroid cancer. Fortunately, it hadn't metastasized. She had her thyroid removed, went on Synthroid, a synthetic thyroid hormone, and had yet another baby with me after that.

At the risk of seeming vain or arrogant, let me ask: Which model of care saved that woman's life? Defensive, institutionalized medicine, or individualized, attentive care?

DOCTORS ARE HARDLY the only ones concerned with safety and saving lives. Like obstetricians, midwives know that just because a woman has a normal pregnancy, it doesn't mean that her baby won't experience fetal distress in labor, that the mother won't hemorrhage after birth, that her placenta won't get stuck and need to be manually removed, or that her baby, who behaved brilliantly all labor long, won't have trouble breathing.

The homebirth midwives with whom I associate in New York City are all equipped to deal with each of these outcomes. I'll venture to say that more often than not, their vast experience can promote patient safety better than the judgment call of a first-year resident, fresh out of medical school, who may be the person attending to the labor floor of a hospital.

Regardless of where a birth takes place, safety is conferred by the ability of the health-care provider to make a quick diagnosis and then to stabilize the patient. This happens as a result of clinical skill and the provider's paying attention, which is where the one-to-one patient-midwife ratio at home wins.

Labor is scary, especially when things aren't going as expected, for both the patient and the practitioner, whether at home, in a hospital, or at a birthing center. Of course, I do my best not to let on about that. I've always been coolheaded under fire; that is until I get to go home and cry, like I did after the first time I resuscitated a baby during a homebirth.

For the sake of my patients, it's a good thing I can hold it together. I do everything I can to quell their fears. I try to tease out their uneasiness and concretize it so we can bring it into consciousness and look at it clearly. I talk to them about which parts of their fears are rational and "irrational." I acknowledge their concerns with humility, but assure them that I have a strategy in place for every single possible unpredictable event. This style of information sharing is a hallmark of my relationships with homebirth patients, and they appreciate it.

That's not to say there is absolutely nothing to be afraid of at all. With birth comes the risk of injury, illness, and even death in every setting, regardless of the careful strategizing and the intelligence and talent of the available practitioners. Sometimes things are completely out of anyone's control.

※

CHAPTER 12

God Bless the Child

IN EVERY SETTING WHERE I have seen birth, I have also seen death. No setting can eradicate that possibility entirely—not a hospital, not a birthing center, not home. Anyone who has practiced this career long enough has experienced an infant life being extinguished, not because of negligence or malpractice or delivering in the wrong place, but because, sadly, babies sometimes die. It's just inevitable.

When I became a midwife, I knew intellectually that infant mortality and morbidity would be part of the equation, but I don't think I could have anticipated what it would feel like to look death in the face.

Attesting to the routineness of death, hospital maternity wards have regular morbidity and mortality rounds, which are meetings to discuss the specifics of cases with bad outcomes. They call it "M and M." But no matter how many times I encounter death, it will never feel routine to me.

I will never get used to it. In over 30 years in this field, I still have not been able to accept it as part of reality. It's just so hard to believe that with all of our fetal monitoring devices, sonograms, and excellent prenatal care, we can't prevent infant death. I'm inclined to try to wish we could, but deep down, I know better. Like it or not, life isn't always fair.

Nothing in life really prepares you for the feelings associated with anyone's passing, least of all that of a newborn. I always find myself feeling sad, angry, betrayed, and helpless, whether I am directly involved in a birth gone bad or just on the outside looking in. Like anyone else, I suppose, I struggle to understand all of the factors that led up to death and agonize over whether doing anything differently might have prevented such an injustice. But there is no solution and little solace rendered by this seemingly futile exercise.

These days, at every birth, I'm on edge the moment when the bluish baby comes through the vagina and breathes or doesn't. I never used to feel that way. Until Lilah.

In 12 years and over 500 deliveries in my private practice, I have lost only one baby. It happened in the summer of 2007, and I am still mourning her loss. I may always mourn for her.

I didn't see it coming. Over the course of my career, I had learned to determine whether there was fetal distress by monitoring the fetal heart rate, and to transfer during labor if there was any. If the baby hadn't experienced distress, I knew with a degree of certainty that even if a baby came out not breathing, I could resuscitate.

Resuscitations had stopped being scary for me. I had been doing them for a long time, and with my success rate at 100 percent, I had developed a high level of confidence. But it wasn't always that way. Early on, the need to resuscitate freaked me out.

As long as I live, I will remember my first solo resuscitation at home, when my practice was new. It happened on the Fourth of July. That was the first baby for whom my breath alone wasn't sufficient. I had to perform chest compressions as well. I was completely alone. There was no one but me, and nothing but my mouth on the baby's mouth and my will desperately urging it to breathe. There was a moment when I didn't know if it would happen. Time froze. But then I saw signs. The baby gasped and tried to get a breath, so I knew I was moving in the right direction. Then the heart rate came up, and the baby started to gain a little color. It wasn't long before the baby let out a long, shrill cry — a sound that brought sweet relief to my heart and mind, as well as to the motionless parents.

I was traumatized after that first resuscitation. When I got home, Liam was there. I was frazzled, and I couldn't really hide it from him. Liam was five or six — young, but not too young for me to explain what had happened in general terms and to teach him about CPR. I told him that what had happened was like the scene in *Jurassic Park* where the kid gets electrocuted on the fence and the dad revives him. It was shortly afterward that I heard Liam brag to his friend Luca that I save people. It was very sweet.

WHEN IT COMES TO DEATH, *A* plus *B* doesn't always equal *C*. Why not? I don't have a clue. I probably never will. I can give excellent prenatal care, make sure a baby doesn't have fetal distress, and transfer if it does. I can keep my skills well honed and updated, and I can keep my pride in check, making sure I'm not keeping a mother at home when things have gotten too rough just so that she can feel victorious and I can feel vindicated. But I have learned, in a way that only experience can teach, that I am not omniscient, nor can I guarantee every outcome just because I care as much as I do and I am conscientious enough to do the right things.

Up until the summer of 2007, I could officially state that I had never had a tragic situation at home. I think on some level, I thought it was avoidable with careful observance and my growing experience with resuscitation. Before then, every baby that came out and didn't breathe, I'd just breathed life into. To date, I have performed such assistance successfully at least 20 times.

An ob-gyn friend and colleague recently shared an interesting story with me. She said she had a friend, an ob-gyn in upstate New York, who had been working for ten years straight without a single bad outcome. Surprisingly, when he went to renew his malpractice insurance, he was denied. Rebuffed by such an injustice, he decided to protest the insurance company's decision. He argued that he was an excellent clinician, as evidenced by his complete lack of fetal loss. Why would he, of all people, be denied coverage? It seemed ridiculous. The insurance company had a different perspective: statistically speaking, they told him, he was due for a loss.

After hearing that story, I couldn't help but wonder: Had I just been due? Had my first infant death been simply a matter of probability?

THE SIMULTANEOUS SURPRISE and inevitability of neonatal death reminds me of the way in which so many women are shocked when they miscarry, even though it is widely known that between 20 and 30 percent of pregnancies end in miscarriage. Questions naturally arise in each woman who goes through it as to why it happened.

I remember one time early in my career, I was dining at a Cuban restaurant on the Upper West Side, and I overheard a woman talking to her girlfriend. In complete despair, she said, "I don't know what I did. I took my vitamins, I drank my milk." I couldn't help but interrupt the conversation and offer this woman some perspective.

I told her what my background was, then offered, "The things you did or didn't do have nothing to do with why you had a miscarriage." I explained that miscarriage is often Mother Nature's triage system, a form of "natural selection" to use Darwin-speak, and told her she shouldn't blame herself. But somehow, even when we know all the probabilities, we all still do.

I have seen this self-blaming again and again. Carrying a baby feels like such a huge responsibility, and as women we try so hard to get everything right. If things don't turn out right, we're all very good at blaming ourselves.

One of my patients experienced a "fetal demise," which is different from both a miscarriage and an infant death. It's when a fetus expires late in the pregnancy but before birth. Once I was working with a woman named Samantha. Her pregnancy had been going well until sometime early in the third trimester, when the baby suddenly wasn't growing well. It's hard to be certain about exactly how well a baby is growing. To be sure, and to put us both at ease, I sent Samantha for a sonogram. According to the results, the baby seemed fine, but the sonographer questioned the conception date and due date, because the baby didn't seem to be the size it should have been. It usually takes two sonograms, two weeks apart, though, to determine whether a baby is indeed not growing, or the dates are just off. Before we had the chance for the second sonogram, Samantha got sick. She was so ill that she couldn't do anything.

The following Monday, Samantha went to meet my backup doctor for a regular prenatal visit, and he couldn't find the baby's heartbeat. I immediately raced her to St. Vincent's. Still no heartbeat. She cried and cried, which is all anyone could do in that moment of learning her baby is gone. But then she started to berate herself, saying that maybe it was because she didn't love the baby enough. I had to set her straight.

I said, "Samantha, there are crackheads who smoke every day and don't love their babies with the care you did, and I've seen their kids be born alive." Actually, a very quirky effect of crack on fetal development is that it contributes to lung maturity by stressing the system, so that a baby born prematurely to a mom on crack might do better in terms of its respiratory status than another baby born prematurely without this drug. Of course, I didn't tell Samantha this. But it's an odd contradiction, no? Granted, the crack often has negative effects on those babies that show up later.

In any case, it wasn't fair or accurate to say that Samantha's baby died because she didn't care about it enough. As a midwife, part of the work I do is provide moms and their partners in this situation with enough information so that they don't trip. It's a delicate piece of the care I give, trying to guide couples from blaming either themselves or each other. Several studies show that losing a child can often stress a relationship to the breaking point.

OVER TIME, I HAVE WITNESSED many neonatal deaths and near-deaths in maternity centers, hospitals, and birthing centers. I consider it part of a professional hazing I had to go through to strengthen me, educate me, and sharpen my skills. Since Lilah passed, I have found myself going over those deaths in my mind many times. Ultimately, the variety of situations reminds me of how unavoidable death is and how it doesn't discriminate. It eventually pays a visit to every practitioner, in every venue, and isn't always preventable with modern conventions like C-sections.

The first neonatal resuscitation I watched was at Melinda's maternity center in El Paso, Texas, mentioned earlier. The baby was born, came out, cried — and then, while lying on the mother's belly, it turned white and passed meconium, which is often a sign of distress in a neonate. I thought it was all over. But, miraculously, right before my eyes, the midwife successfully resuscitated that baby.

Years later, at the Allen Pavilion, a doctor I worked with accepted a patient into labor and delivery while she was in early labor, because the woman broke her water and discovered thick meconium. When she was just two centimeters dilated, the doctor sectioned her. It didn't matter, though; the baby didn't make it.

In a few places, I've seen mothers come in to the hospital on their due date with no risk factors but no fetal movement — and no heartbeat.

At the birthing center, one mother was fully dilated when she passed thick black meconium. Her midwife transferred her to the hospital within 22 minutes. The mom arrived at the hospital with the baby in her tummy. But it was still, and it had no heartbeat. An autopsy showed it had coarctation of the aorta, a congenital heart anomaly.

I ENCOUNTERED A CONGENITAL heart defect in another baby I delivered. I remember this one very clearly, not just because of the heart anomaly but because it involved being pulled away from Liam as I so often am. It was at a time when all of my patients for the month had delivered, so I thought I was free to spend some quality time with him. Liam is a total chocoholic, and I got invited to this chocolate show somewhere on West 17th Street. I was so excited to bring Liam to that show. He was around seven at the time.

I knew he would enjoy it, and I had been longing for some mother-son bonding. But first I had to go to New Jersey for a postpartum visit with one of my patients, so Geoff was going to bring him to the chocolate show and I'd meet them there. After my appointment, I headed straight to West 17th Street. As I was circling the block, I saw Liam and Geoff standing in line. I waved to them excitedly. And then my pager went off. So what else is new?

It was one of Miriam's patients. Just as Miriam covers for me when more than one mother delivers on the same day, I sometimes cover for her. It doesn't happen that often, but when it does, I've got to fly.

It killed me to leave. Here I was, so excited to share this experience with my kid, and the moment got ripped from my grasp. I got on the phone with Jenna, the doula I love so much, who was there with the mother.

I said, "Jenna, do I really need to come right now? Is it time?"

And Jenna said, "Yes."

It was one of those moments where I just have to flip a switch emotionally. I have to be a grown-up — and ask my kid to be kind of a grown-up — and shift right into duty mode.

It broke my heart telling Liam I couldn't stay. I drove up next to him and Geoff as they were waiting in line in the rain and sadly told them the news. They were already pretty used to this kind of thing, and they just resolved to go in without me. I took comfort that they would have fun together — that Liam at least had his dad.

On top of my disappointment, my stomach was grumbling. I hadn't had a chance to eat. The mother who was delivering lived on the Upper West Side, so I thought about stopping at the McDonald's (my favorite fine-dining experience) on the corner of 71st and Broadway on my way.

I called Jenna and said, "I'm so hungry. Do I have a second to get something to eat first?"

And she said, "No, Cara. The mother is pushing." So I went directly there.

When I got to the apartment, the mother was in the pool. I checked the baby's heartbeat. I thought, *I need to eat for the greater good of everyone here. If I don't have any energy, it's not going to be good for anyone.* I checked the fridge for something to eat, but it was all spring water and wheatgrass in there. And I got the evil eye from the mother for even checking it out.

I went back to the mother. She was standing up between contractions, then squatting down and pushing in the pool. She wasn't happy that I wasn't Miriam. She was angry and frustrated that the person she'd been able to rely on so far, the woman to whom she'd given all her soulful trust, couldn't be there for her. During one of her pushes, I took a gloved hand and put it down underneath her, just barely touching her vulva to feel if the head was emerging. It wasn't. I tried to calm her. I said, "Good, good. Everything's fine."

And she snapped, "That's my clitoris!" I was insulted. As if I didn't know what I was doing. She had thought that I couldn't possibly get an idea of her progress without doing a vaginal exam. But of course that simple placement of the hand gave me all the information I needed to encourage her to continue pushing.

So there I was, doing my job after sacrificing a day with my son for a mom who didn't trust me because I wasn't who she wanted to be there. She didn't like me because she met me at the height of her pain and vulnerability. She didn't think I could do a proper vaginal exam because I saved her the discomforts of a typical vaginal exam. And she didn't want me to eat her food.

I was also in the wrong clothes. I was dressed for leisure, for going to a chocolate show with my son, in funky jeans with designs on them. I wasn't dressed for birth. Usually I wear very basic, toned-down stretch clothes that allow me to get on all fours and help my moms without feeling too constricted. But on that day, I hadn't had time to change, so I wasn't looking too professional, which didn't help matters.

I remember getting a look of solace from Jenna. She knew I had just walked into a difficult situation. Her look of support helped me stay focused on what I needed to do.

I kept listening to the baby on the Doppler between contractions, and it had a great heartbeat. It seemed to be doing fine in utero: there were no decelerations, and there was no meconium. But when the baby came out, it did not breathe. I had to do a full-blown resuscitation.

Jenna brought me the bulb syringe, and I went to tilt the baby's head back, but the mother kept trying to keep the baby away from me. It's a totally normal maternal reaction, but it was getting in the way of saving the baby's life. There was the mother in the pool, holding on to her baby for dear life, thinking I was trying to submerge it or something. She finally let me do what I needed to do, which included some mouth-to-mouth and CPR. The baby came around.

Later, when Miriam came by, I took her aside and told her to listen to the baby's heart carefully. "It just doesn't make any sense that this baby crashed," I told her.

Sure enough, the pediatrician discovered on exam, the baby had a congenital heart anomaly. It died a month later in surgery. Poor thing. Poor mom. Even with all the grief she has suffered as a result of her loss, she still recognizes and has expressed that if her baby had been born in the hospital, and the defect picked up immediately, she may not have had her daughter for her first month of life.

WHILE I WITNESSED every one of those cases, they weren't mine. Lilah was mine. Her safety was in my hands, and I took that very seriously, as always.

Lilah of the night, still and gray in my hands, why won't you breathe when I blow into you first with my mouth and then with the Ambu Bag I keep handy for just such instances. Why is your heart not beating when I just heard it two minutes ago with the Doppler? Why is Joan, another homebirth midwife, here to witness this dark, empty moment with the parents wailing? Why do I still have my son? Why did my friend Debbie Miller get out of her car on a dark Vermont highway to lend assistance to two women trapped in their car after they crashed, only to get hit by a truck? I am exhausted by my incomprehension of these events.

Sometimes I find it hard to handle such huge responsibility, and I just want to quit.

HERE'S LILAH'S STORY.

Lisa was my last mom to deliver before I went on my August vacation. I was headed for Paris for part of the time and was going to Costa Rica for the rest. Liam was at camp. I had the luxury of time and the knowledge that there couldn't possibly be a conflict with another delivery, since my other patients had all delivered and I didn't have any others lined up until September. I could spend all the time I needed with Lisa.

She had hired a wonderful, grounded, and experienced doula named Sarah. Sarah had delivered two babies at home, her first in Colorado and her last with me in Brooklyn. With Jenna in nursing school and unavailable, I had been working mostly with Sarah, who's just great.

When I went to Lisa's last few prenatal visits, she was completely sick of being pregnant, as most of us are when we go late. It was mid-July, and the heat can be very hard during pregnancy. Legs swell and sluggishness sets in from carrying around all that extra weight. She was at 41-plus weeks. The baby was moving and a perfect size, presenting head down.

We decided at our prenatal visit, that since she would reach 42 weeks on Monday, which would bring about the need for a trip to the hospital and fetal evaluation for postdates, that it was just as savvy a plan to try to urge Lilah out before she reached that mark.

This was our plan. Friday night, I went over and evaluated Lilah's heartbeat as a precaution before we would begin the induction. I would sweep Lisa's membranes — move my finger around her cervix to separate the amniotic membranes from the lower uterine segment, which stimulates the release of the hormone prostaglandin, which can kick-start labor — and then Lisa would take some castor oil to move things along a little more.

At 7 PM, she took the castor oil. Contractions began around 10:30 PM. I went over around 3 AM. I was being so cautious with this baby, mostly because Lisa had been nervous, and her anxiety somehow spread to me. I wanted to calm myself.

I listened to the baby when Lisa's contractions first started. They were regular and painful but in the latent phase. By 7 AM, I had listened to the baby for four hours almost continuously, and at that point was feeling ridiculous that we were even intervening before the 42-week mark, because everything was in such great shape. When labor slowed down a little, I went home to sleep and let Lisa get some shut-eye, too. After a little rest, we would see what her body would do on its own.

Sarah, the doula, went over in the morning and kept Lisa company and in good spirits. They walked around. The contractions were erratic. This didn't worry me. I have now had a lot of moms with labors that start and stop over the course of a few days until they finally get going. We call this prodromal labor. If a woman is planning a hospital birth, she is sent home from the hospital to fend for herself when this happens. But not Lisa. She was well attended by her adorable husband, Jordan, her mom, Sarah, and me. We all checked in on her throughout the day and were all completely available to her.

I went back to her place around 5 that evening. We decided to help the baby's head further into the pelvis by wrapping her belly with a scarf. In this way the baby's bottom couldn't fall forward and bring the head off of the cervix, where it was needed to enhance dilation. This way, we could hopefully speed things along and get this baby out. Lisa's contractions had slowed, so we once more gave her a small amount of castor oil and went for a walk.

After walking for two hours, Lisa's labor was booming again. We came home, still listening to Lilah's heart-beat. There was not a deceleration in sight. And this time, it looked like Lisa's labor would keep going. We all took turns supporting her emotionally, with Jordan and Sarah in the lead. I was busy checking Lilah's heartbeat on a regular basis.

Everyone got tired, so as is the homebirth way, we each took a turn helping Lisa while the others rested. I volunteered to stay with Lisa and support her from about 3 AM until 7 AM. Sarah was lying on a mattress on the floor in the same room I was in. Lisa's mom and hubby were in the other room trying to get some sleep. And valiant Lisa was on her hands and knees on the bed during contractions and lying forward on some pillows or on her side between them. When she was at rest, I would place the Doppler on her abdomen and hear the comforting *byk e byk e byk* sound. The heartbeat was in the 130s and steady. All good.

In the wee hours of the morning, Lisa's water broke with light meconium. Light meconium can mean a lot of things, but in general, to me, it means that I now have to watch the baby more carefully, if that was even possible, and that if I hear decelerations of the heart rate, we should probably consider transferring. We didn't hear any such thing.

When dawn broke, I realized that Lisa had not voided in a while and I could both palpate and observe a full bladder, which is typical if the baby is in an occiput posterior presentation with the baby's head down but facing the mother's abdomen. This position is often associated with longer labor, which is what I had been thinking was the case for Lisa all along. Of course, I have a catheter for that purpose, one that I sterilize for subsequent use. The only problem was that I had sterilized this one really well, so well that it was not patent any longer, meaning it was sealed shut. Nothing could go through it. I tried to cut it down, looking for an open area while still keeping it long enough to function, but I had no luck.

Lisa had a friend who offered to go to the pharmacy to get another. But it was 7-ish, and the pharmacy didn't open until 8 o'clock. I wasn't sure I wanted to wait that long, so I called my old buddy and colleague Joan. Joan, in her helpful way, asked me if I wanted her to bring one over. I said yes. She did.

Up until then, Lisa's vaginal exams had shown a persistent cervical lip. This is another common occurrence in an occiput posterior presentation. Lisa had instinctively chosen to be on her hands and knees, a position that would reduce the lip. By the time Joan arrived, with just a touch of pushing, Lisa had rotated the baby into occiput anterior position — with the baby's head facing her back — a more common presentation, often associated with shorter labor. Things began to move forward rather quickly. We emptied Lisa's bladder with the fresh catheter, and there we were. Joan had brought some fresh energy, Lisa had turned the head into a better position as evidenced by progress of descent, and we were in the pushing stage. We'd turned the corner after a long night.

Lilah came down quickly, as often happens after a stall caused by occiput posterior positioning. Once the baby rotates, things move quickly. I continued monitoring the baby between pushes, which is how I can determine whether the baby is having any difficulty in this stage. It's normal to have some decelerations at this point because of head compression. The bones in the baby's head are being compressed as it passes through the mother's bones on the way out. Deceleration can also occur if there is a cord around the neck. But there were no decelerations. The baby was clearly doing well.

That is, until we could see three inches of her head gently stretching out Lisa's perineum. She then had a deceleration to 60 beats per minute. I didn't like it, and my gut knew that something wasn't right. This was odd because I have been at many deliveries where babies have had decelerations of this nature, even more than one without incident. One woman, whom I eventually took to the hospital, had hours and hours of decels once she was in the hospital. The doctor finally sectioned her only as a precaution so as to not leave the baby for hours in a potentially compromising situation. Of course the baby was fine: attaining a 9 at one minute and a 10 at five minutes on the Apgar scale, which evaluates a baby's adaptation to extrauterine life immediately following the birth. In situations like that, it's hard not to feel as though the mother holds me accountable for an unnecessary C-section.

So here we were on the frontier of triumph with Lilah, but we had this one decel that was causing me concern. I felt her kick. I didn't like it. Lisa felt her kick, too, and said so. I told Lisa we had to get her out *right then*. Lisa pushed like crazy and out she came, still as the night.

I gently told Mom and Dad not to worry, that a baby who had behaved that well in labor would come around, and I began resuscitating. I had already pulled the oxygen and Ambu Bag within my reach before the birth. I was lucky to have Joan nearby, who prepared the Ambu Bag and oxygen, while I cleared Lilah's airway. I immediately began resuscitating.

Usually, when I resuscitate babies, they begin to gasp and the heartbeat comes up from less than 60 to over 80 then over 100, and then we're out of the woods. Usually, breaths alone, either through mouth-to-mouth or from an Ambu Bag, result in success. But there was no longer anything usual about this situation.

The resuscitation wasn't working. I gave the Ambu Bag to Joan, who kept bagging the baby while I continued doing chest compressions. The paramedics who had come didn't do anything more helpful. All the while, the family was wailing in a way I will never forget. The feeling that I would never be able to forgive myself started manifesting. Never. It was accompanied by the feeling of *Why me?* Why had everything I had counted on, that had worked for the last 20 years, failed? I still don't get it.

I continued bagging and doing CPR in the back of the ambulance all the way to the hospital, but I knew this would end gravely. I mean, how long do babies have before no oxygen to the brain becomes an issue? The official limit used to be considered four to five minutes. Then it was changed to ten minutes. We had passed both of those limits.

Suddenly, all our lives — the parents', the grandparents', the doula's, and mine — were turned upside down. We all started analyzing what we might have missed or could have done differently. We all had to ask ourselves if this baby would have been alive if indeed she had been born in the hospital. And the truth is that we will never know the answer to that question.

EVERYONE GRIEVES UNIQUELY. There is no right way to do it, and we all have a hard time getting through it. The level of heartache at the beginning of the grieving process is excruciating; it's virtually unbearable. It only even begins to recede with time. The mental anguish can be overwhelming, too. That part is especially pronounced for me, as the practitioner in this case. I have racked my brain again and again, trying to ascertain just what went wrong. One aspect of homebirth I had never considered before was how hard it is emotionally for the midwife when death occurs. There is no team of people with whom to commiserate. The burden of responsibility and understanding falls exclusively on me.

Initially, it was hard not to doubt my judgment about everything. For weeks and months, and even still, I revisited every single thought process and action taken over the course of Lisa's labor. But, strangely, every time I've questioned myself, people have come out of the woodwork with facts and anecdotes that remind me that I had taken great pains to do everything with proper care.

That very week, a midwife and a physician both told me stories of their losses. The midwife told me about a mom in the hospital who got out of bed for a second to use the bathroom, and when she returned to the bed, there was no fetal heart rate on the monitor. One of my backup perinatologists told me about another baby in the hospital who died after being continuously monitored.

Everywhere I turned in despair and self-recrimination, people told me stories that did not support that recrimination. These stories were like a soft wind that spoke gently to me, saying, *You know you did everything to take care of that baby.*

The same thing happened for the parents. Everywhere they went, professionals shared their stories of similar deaths in the hospital. No one exploited the line of thinking that this might not have happened if only the baby had been born in the hospital. And the parents didn't blame me. This sort of grace strikes me as unusual. I am grateful for it.

It was remarkable to me how without knowing anything about what I had been through, people, like angels, appeared to alleviate my sense of guilt about Lilah's death. I remember one phone call I placed to the state phenylketonuria (PKU) testing unit. Their department had attempted to contact Lisa to let her know that one of her baby's PKU results was out of whack and that she would need to do a retest. I wanted to investigate whether there was a connection between this wayward lab result and the baby's death.

While I was telling the woman who answered the phone about this, she said, "Oh I'm so sorry. That must be so hard for you." She was unusually kind, especially considering she didn't know me. I suppose I assumed that because she worked for a state agency overseeing an aspect of birth, she would have felt compelled to pass judgment, especially since it was a homebirth. But, no. This woman had had a homebirth herself in the 1980s and had nothing but kind words for me. With a homebirth rate of only about 1 percent, what were the odds that I would be connected with this home-birth-friendly woman on an anonymous phone call to the Department of Newborn Screening?

Another strangely synchronistic occurrence happened during a phone call I made to a dog breeder in upstate New York. I was calling to find out about the teacup Yorkies that she was selling, because my son was ready to get a dog. When she found out that I was a midwife, she was so thrilled, and she began telling me — with no knowledge of what I had just been through — that she knew there was so much responsibility involved with being present at a birth and that it was such a relief to talk to someone else in this position. She was the midwife for her dogs, she explained, and then launched into talking about how hard it is when some pups come out and don't make it. Why on earth, I wondered, was she talking about this kind of stuff with no knowledge of my experience?

It felt a lot like someone — God, the forces that be, *someone* — wanted me not to blame myself, the same force that wanted me to live the night in nursing school when I was attacked at gunpoint in Riverdale and received the message that the gun was a prop. These small moments helped me to move gradually toward forgiving myself. They brought me a new perspective: a bottom-line realization that I can take my responsibility very seriously — and I do — but that doesn't mean that I can always prevent death.

AFTER WE LOST LILAH, I was completely torn about going to Paris. But I knew that there was nothing more I could do for Lisa and Jordon. They knew they had my full support. I had spent a lot of time with them, and I decided to check in by phone and email while I was away.

I met my sister Kim in Paris. I couldn't help but think that she was the one to whom I said that if anything happened to me at Liam's birth, to make sure no one blamed Miriam.

I had many a dark, numb night in Paris, oblivious to the city itself. I still think about Lilah most nights as I lie down in the dark. Kim was wonderful on our trip. A therapist, she was very attentive and perceptive and helped me to talk about the event in a way that was cathartic and comforting.

Although Kim's hand-holding was very helpful to me during this difficult time, I found I needed to spend some time alone before going back to work in September. I took the second half of my vacation with Liam in Costa Rica, where I did a lot of thinking. I was welcomed there, with open arms, by my good friends Bismark and Gloria. They noticed right away that I wasn't my usual happy-go-lucky self. I let them in on what I had been going through, and Gloria, in turn, opened up to me. She told me about how she had lost her only son in childbirth after having two daughters and that she would probably not have any more children. She talked to me about the pain she experienced when her baby died and how, after a difficult struggle, she eventually came to accept his death.

When I got back home, I tried to process the death experience with my therapist. She told me that years ago, there was a psychic who said that some babies on the way out change their mind about being born and their hearts just fail. I liked that idea. I shared that anecdote with Lisa, and she liked it, too. Later, when I reviewed the case with a perinatologist who's a colleague, he suggested that maybe it was a cord accident, implying that the baby may have pressed on the cord on the way out, cutting off its oxygen supply. I found a different kind of comfort in this explanation, and I thought Lisa might, too. But when I told her, she started crying and said she liked the psychic's explanation better. Maybe Lilah had changed her mind on the way out.

I felt so horrible to have upset Lisa like that. But that's what I mean about everyone's unique experiences of grieving: She had different lessons to learn than I did. For me, the understanding that it might not have been a preventable death gave me comfort, as I faced the ultimate responsibility to bring that baby safely into the world. But Lisa's perspective as Lilah's mom was from a completely different place.

So we grieved differently and yet together, staying in close contact. I made it a point to gather all the records in case Lisa ever had questions at some point in the future regarding any postmortem information we might have discovered that could make a difference if she decided to have another baby. Last we spoke, she is not interested in researching. I completely understand.

✳

CHAPTER 13

Cinema Maternismo

AFTER LILAH'S PASSING, I was a little bit nervous about jumping back into work. Ironically, the first birth I had that September was with a mom who preferred that I not listen to the fetal heartbeat very often. I remember pretty much having to implore her to let me listen between pushes, telling her that descent is when the baby is most likely to experience distress. She reluctantly allowed me. In hindsight, I realize that her assumption that everything was okay, and that it would continue to be, helped take the heat off my bruised clinical confidence.

I don't think I was actually aware of how negatively I was affected by Lilah's death until I had a labor and delivery that followed a very similar path as hers. It was a long labor, Claudia's first. After having had prodomal, or latent labor, for about a day, and after we'd had many conversations on the phone, I knew that she would feel better if I just checked in on her to see how she was doing and administer some face-to-face, heart-to-heart reassurance.

I reluctantly gave up my parking space on a Saturday night. It was 7 PM, and I knew that I'd be arriving back home in time for the weekend revelers from uptown, the outer boroughs, and the suburbs to have grabbed all the eligible parking in my neighborhood. But I felt compelled to go.

After a reassuring evaluation in which prodromal labor was confirmed, I encouraged Claudia to get some rest with the help of Ambien and I headed home. Claudia's doula stayed with her, coaching her through this phase of labor. Things seemed okay.

Then, at 4:30 AM, Claudia paged, reporting rupture of membranes — translation: Her water had broken. And she had an urge to push. Back I went.

When I arrived, though, she was still in the latent phase. It seemed like just a normal long primip labor. We continued to wait for it to be over, all the while joining Claudia through her fair share of walking. Toward the end, there was some light meconium. I thought, *Uh-oh*. I realized I could wait some more — although with meconium, it's best to get things going — or I could have her push the baby's head around to the occiput anterior position exactly as Lisa had done with Lilah. I suddenly realized I was stuck at the same juncture I had been at with Lisa.

Of course, Claudia was eagerly anticipating my direction. Just a little effort, in terms of turning the baby's head, would get things done. But I was frozen. I decided to call

Val, a good friend and an experienced midwife, and run my thoughts and feelings by her. I told Val how much the labor resembled Lisa's and how much I felt stuck in my own fears, wary of making a judgment call I had made hundreds of times before with confidence. Val offered to come to the birth, even if it meant being present just for my sake. I took her up on her offer, and she was there in a flash.

As soon as I knew Val was on her way, Claudia began pushing. Within a half hour, shortly after Val walked in, Claudia birthed her little girl, who was fully breathing. I will be eternally grateful to Val for coming that day. It made me realize how important support is to everyone involved in childbirth, midwives included.

NOT LONG AFTER THAT, one of my moms, Daphne Beal, published an article in *Vogue* about her wonderful experience with the homebirth of her second child, Mira, after having delivered her first child in the hospital. Daphne had had a beautiful homebirth, the kind where the parents, the doula, and the midwife are all toasting with champagne flutes within an hour of the birth, while the baby happily snuggles at the breast.

In the months before the article came out, I was still in a fairly dark place. Daphne had been emailing me about final revisions. She didn't know of my recent experience with Lilah, and I wasn't sure that it would be appropriate on any level to share it with her, so I kept skipping over her emails, avoiding answering them, until I realized that it was only fair to respond to her questions and not hold up the process. It felt too strange to be involved in celebrating the glorious side of homebirth while the darker side was engulfing me. So, reluctantly, in an email to Daphne, I finally opened up about my first infant death at home. She was so understanding of the feelings I had and insisted that it was a good idea to add that statistic — my 1 infant loss in more than 700 births — to the article.

I was unsure of what to do and called my professional organization, the American College of Nurse-Midwives (ACNM) to get some helpful advice. I was worried that opponents of homebirth would have a field day and that my own patients might forever lose their faith in this very viable option, not to mention their trust in me as a midwife. Daphne assured me that I could trust her judgment, pointing out that it didn't seem realistic for a midwife with my level of experience to have never had a bad outcome. Around the same time, one of my patients, with whom I am very close, told me on the phone that she figured I would have had at least a couple of infant deaths by this point in my career. I let Daphne put it in the article, and I have come to feel good that the truth is out there.

When the article came out, I realized that an important part of my healing process was acknowledging all the women who, like Daphne, had put their trust in me and experienced positive outcomes. I had just been through a serious but inevitable hazing. While it could have destroyed me, I saw that I couldn't let it. I needed to begin to recover and see the experience as a step toward my maturation as a midwife who now truly knew that in spite of everything — my skills, my judgment calls, my love for my patients — I cannot guarantee perfection.

It was good timing, because I was about to be thrust into the spotlight again with the premiere of *The Business of Being Born,* a documentary in which I am featured attending births in 2006 and 2007 and giving birth to Liam in 1995.

IT WAS KIND OF SURREAL to get a call from Ricki Lake in 2006 inviting me to participate in the documentary that ultimately became *The Business of Being Born.* Did I ever think that I would meet, or even just speak on the phone, with Ricki Lake, the actress and talk show host? Nope.

Early in my practice, a patient recommended my services to Cindy Crawford when she was considering a homebirth. When I didn't hear from her, I figured I wasn't going to be a midwife to the stars, and I was perfectly fine with that. It turns out I hadn't heard from her because she moved back to Los Angeles. Little did I know that my association with celebrities was merely postponed.

Ironically, my connection to the celebrity world, my svengali if you will, is the hardworking, spotlight-shunning, unassuming Miriam. She has been such an important driving force in the New York City homebirth scene. In our peer group, she was the first one to dare to take the plunge into homebirth. Despite her pioneering ways, she never claimed a competitive edge. Instead, she always fostered and supported the growth of new practices, mine included. At least two midwives who are currently practicing homebirth here began their midwifery education as a result of their own homebirths with her. Miriam was my midwife, and she was Ricki's midwife, too. Ricki was so moved by her experience at home with Miriam that she was inspired to devote her passion, energy, and funds to the production of this film.

I used to tease Miriam about being a midwife for celebrities. It's not surprising that she attracts such discerning, well-heeled patients. She's very smart, and although she's a wisp of a woman, she possesses a startling power to transform. One of her first assistants, Jan, used to say that she thought Miriam had been a switchboard operator in another life because of her natural schmoozing abilities. She is a master on the phone. Her convictions and charisma have given many women the courage to choose homebirth with confidence. It's funny — she has always naturally attracted special people and things to her. She and I have known each other for so many years now as friends and colleagues. When we used to shop at the Salvation Army together, which we often did, she would somehow always come across the only Lanvin dress among racks of secondhand Gap shirts. A celebrity clientele, therefore, was no surprise.

She was originally supposed to be featured in the movie the way I eventually was. But when Ricki had approached her, Miriam was already on a sort of sabbatical in Africa. So she sent Ricki my way, and chose to remain in the shadows.

But if the viewer watches *The Business of Being Born* carefully, her loving hands appear and her voice can be heard, at both my and Ricki's births. The ability to remain unseen and not only to allow the birthing woman to have her power, but to help her achieve it, instead of stealing that spotlight, is what makes a midwife (Miriam, in this case) amazing.

The whole experience of making the film was very strange and exciting for me. I remember agreeing to meet Abby Epstein, the director, at the Ciao for Now café in my neighborhood, on East 12th Street, with an uncomfortable feeling in my gut. It turned out that she and her boyfriend, Paolo Netto, the cinematographer for the movie, also lived in the East Village. Before meeting her, I was haunted by the suspicions of dubious intentions that usually arise in me around endeavors involving voyeurism into what is a very private event. I generally don't approve of that sort of intrusion into the very personal and sacred experience of birth by people so far outside of it, so I thought I might not want to participate in the movie.

Aside from any potential feelings of invasion of privacy among families that might be filmed, I was also concerned about how midwifery would be portrayed in the movie. There's always the fear that the journalists exploring the subject might not look deeply enough to get the true story, and that they instead might latch onto just one aspect of homebirth and re-amplify stereotypes that we've been trying so hard to fight.

That's what happened when Miriam was profiled in the *New York Times* in 1998. In the end, the reporter emphasized how people who choose homebirth tend to like astrology and shop at the food co-op. I couldn't believe it. They were still portraying the proponents of homebirth as hippies or *macha* women with a higher pain threshold than most of the rest of us who would never make such a choice and give up their shot at an epidural.

Another journalist at the *New York Times* interviewed me for a 2005 article on homebirth that ran in the Metro section. For some reason, that reporter used little more from our interview than a quote from me about my idea for a budget birthing pool. Lord knows I had said many pithier things about empowerment and other aspects of homebirth, but that's what the paper went with. I read that article and felt once again, *Are these people for real?* They have come so close to such a huge, sacred event, with such immense political repercussions, and then profaned it, oversimplified it, and reduced it once again to the black and white of one of the usual themes: those who choose homebirth do so to prove that they don't need the establishment. To them, it's some sort of crusade of rebellion against pain medication that somehow involves healthy eating. People who oversimplify homebirth miss the real meat of the matter.

BUT WHEN I MET WITH ABBY, I was pleasantly surprised by her gentle intelligence and her sense that the film could hold some cultural import. I remember feeling that the moment we met was completely synchronistic, as I had been fantasizing that Kate, my apprentice, and I would someday be able to make our own documentary about homebirth, setting many a record straight. Now, after having been involved in the movie and having witnessed how much work it was for Abby and her team, I laugh at the notion of my trying to make a movie. Yeah, in all my spare time. Very funny.

By the time Abby had finished introducing her idea, I told her how happy I was that someone was finally going to make the movie I'd been dreaming about making — someone who was a real filmmaker! I couldn't believe the rightness of the feeling.

Abby and her crew were completely professional and sensitive in every way, from the fliers they created to introduce my patients to the idea of being filmed for the movie, to the way that Abby would meet with couples in person and on the phone once I had presented them with the idea and prepped them. This way, she had made personal contact with them, which is so important in the homebirth arena. It seemed as if Abby understood she'd have to earn their trust. A director who didn't understand the type of trust and commitment required to enter the arena of homebirth wouldn't be able to get very good footage. I think that because Ricki had been through homebirth herself, she might have had an influence on this aspect of Abby's understanding.

To add to my comfort level, Ricki mentioned that Abby had directed *V-Day: Until the Violence Stops,* a documentary about the making of *The Vagina Monologues* and the awareness the play has brought to the issue of violence against women. I rented the documentary to get an idea of how Abby had dealt with an issue as sensitive as abuse, and she had done it beautifully. I would say that watching the way women were interviewed with such respect about an uncomfortable topic like sexual abuse gave me another hunch that Abby would do a great job with the subject of homebirth. In *V-Day,* she never got in the way or trivialized the women's deeper feelings. I felt that was important. I felt more and more at ease with the idea of the project. It was nice to feel sure that I'd be portrayed accurately and it was nice not to feel like I was going to be somehow taken down in the process.

WE HAD GREAT CHEMISTRY. It didn't hurt that Abby and Paolo were longtime East Villagers like me. They were also great with Liam. I loved how they interacted with him when they first met; they were warm, friendly, and playful. Ah, a mother's weakness — treat her kid well and she'll do almost anything for you! We chose a familiar neighborhood restaurant as our out-of-work meeting place, Takahachi, a great sushi place on Avenue A, which is also Liam's favorite restaurant. We still get together there, even though our work on the film is long behind us.

It's a good thing we got along as well as we did, because we spent a lot of time together. Abby and Paolo and their crew followed me around a lot over the course of a little more than a year. They went with me in the car to prenatal calls and to a few births. When we drove together, Paolo would always sit in the passenger seat with a gigantic hand-held camera pointed directly at me.

Abby would be in the backseat trying to make up for the fact that I couldn't speak intelligibly on command. Ready, okay go ahead! "Uuhhhhh..." She would always have pro-vocative questions at the ready to get me talking. I guess my best thoughts come out when I'm not feeling self-conscious. No wonder I understand birthing women as well as I do. Paolo laughingly said that they got their best stuff out of me when I was talking on the cell phone in the car, because then I was completely unaware of him and the camera.

I loved being part of a team, and with Abby and Paolo, it really did feel like a team effort. They were very tuned in to me and my patients. If a woman didn't want her birth filmed, Abby and Paolo never pressured her. Those who did choose to be filmed felt really good about it. In retrospect, it's hard to believe that the film crew could be somewhat unnoticeable inside someone's home, but they really were. Having the vibe is everything, and they were very low-key. I found it easy to ignore them when they were filming because the events and feelings of birth are so dominant. It did help that they maintained a very quiet, respectful presence.

I hope tickets for moving violations cannot be issued retroactively. If so, the movie provides the traffic police with a lot of proof of my talking on the phone while driving. In fact, as is shown in the movie, I also possess the remarkable talent of being able to talk on my cell while driving with my right elbow and holding a map with my left hand. It's a skill that highlights my multitasking ability. Since the film was shot, my Subaru bit the dust, which left me no choice but to buy a Toyota Prius with a navigation system and Bluetooth. So I'm totally kosher now. I feel like Knight Rider. I'm talking to the dashboard on a regular basis instead of putting myself at risk for an accident, as people who see the movie often seem to be concerned about. I promise, there's no more driving with the cell phone up to my ear and a map on the steering wheel.

But I do remember doing just that one night on the way to a birth in lower Westchester County for a Jewish Orthodox woman named Rebecca. She desperately wanted to get the birth out of the way before *Pessach,* or Passover, so she took castor oil against my advice to start labor. Of course, she called me way too late, after the castor oil had sped things up. So I had to be on the cell phone reporting the play-by-play of my arrival. "Okay Rebecca, I'm coming around the corner, I'm pulling into the driveway," etc.

While driving, I also coached Rebecca through blowing — *whooh whooh whooh whooh* — as she tried to hold back from pushing. I got to her just barely in time for the birth. Rebecca hadn't confessed to using the castor oil, and after the birth, I let her know that I was on to her. But I wasn't too hard on her because, in a way, I love that she had the gumption and personal power to just do it the way she wanted to.

IN THE MOVIE, I REALIZE there's a lot of ironic, almost pathetic, humor in my driving frantically to births and in my many parking woes. Katie, my assistant, is always laughing at antics that she finds funny, such as the fact that I get so many tickets and insist on not paying them if they are unfair, even while the authorities proceed to suspend my license. I'm not going to pay for a ticket given to me unjustly for passing a guy driving five miles an hour and going over the double yellow line while on the way to a homebirth! I don't care! Those are my priorities. If I had special plates and a siren like the ambulances do, it would be a different story.

In light of the work I do and the devotion with which I do it, one would think I would have better car karma. My car would always start. It would never be broken into, so my work clothes and birthing equipment would never get stolen. The parking gods would smile upon me, orchestrating the flow of traffic in such a way that there would always be a convenient, legal spot just waiting for me after I've navigated the jammed streets of New York City on my way to make house calls to expectant mothers.

Unfortunately, this is not the case. Part of the reality of being a homebirth midwife in New York City is that I am always contending with car issues, fighting parking tickets, reclaiming my car after it's been towed, and having my license suspended because I haven't had a chance to go to fight my tickets in a timely fashion.

I can't afford a $400-a-month parking spot, and even if I could, there isn't a lot close enough to my home and office for me to be able to access it as quickly as I often need to. The problem is, I don't have special license plates. Diplomats, clergy, newspaper reporters — they all have special plates for their cars that exempt them from parking rules, especially in cases of emergency. But not midwives. Never mind that we are delivering babies and, often, saving lives. The lack of special plates is not just an inconvenience — it's a reflection of midwives' larger issues. One day I'm going to go down to City Hall and say, "Hey! I'm a homebirth midwife. I need special plates!"

Till then, I'll have to keep putting up with a lot of car-related aggravation. Like the time I took Lynn Fisher, another midwife, to do my Tuesday Brooklyn rounds of prenatal visits in women's homes. At our first appointment, we double-parked like everyone else does during street cleaning hours. Unfortunately, the appointment went longer than expected. We didn't get out until it was past the allotted time for double-parking. Sure enough, the car was towed — with my birth equipment in it and all of Lynn's stuff, including her cell phone. That would never have happened if I had special plates.

I called the Parking Violations Bureau's hotline to find out where the car had been taken, and I got some sort of no-information, fuck-you message about their computers being down and please call back tomorrow. We asked a passing livery cab driver for help, and he told us just to go to the

Brooklyn Navy Yard because that's where all the towed cars wind up.

But first, we had another appointment. The livery driver took us to the next mama. I had to act like it was normal not to have my car containing my birth equipment, even though the patient was due any minute. I didn't want to make her panic. She must have thought it was odd that I needed to use her phone to call a cab at the end of her visit, since I usually just hop in the car and drive away.

Lynn and I took that same cab to the Brooklyn Navy Yard. A lot of harsh orders and $185 later, we had the car and all of our stuff back, though not before Lynn slipped on some ice and scraped her knee. But that didn't stop her from showing up the next day for our second day of prenatal visits, which went much better. She proved herself to be a trouper — definitely homebirth material.

There have been flat tires at the peak of labor. I've been pulled over for driving while talking on my cell phone — although, one time, a woman officer was so awed by the work I do, she let me go. My car has been broken into more than once. I have a good laugh imagining what some street thug would do with my speculum. Maybe use the kellies — the clamps I use in cutting the umbilical cord — as roach clips? And what's the street value of Pitocin?

One time, I got to my car and found an older man taking my birthing equipment, birthing clothes and a PlayStation I had bought for a friend's kids out of the car and piling it up on the sidewalk.

"Hey! What do you think you're doing?" my friend demanded.

I was aghast. I couldn't afford to lose all that stuff, to not have it the minute I needed it — which could be any minute.

"Listen," I told the man very calmly but sternly, "do you know what I do for a living? I have to help women give birth to babies in their homes. There's no one but me who can help them. So if I get called now to go to a birth and I don't have my oxygen, and a baby dies because I don't have that oxygen — because you're robbing my car — that's going to be on your conscience."

Shaking, he said, "I'm sorry." Then he started quietly putting my things back in the car, one by one. I offered him the PlayStation, but he wouldn't take it.

Clearly, I got through to that guy. Now if only I could get through to the Parking Violations Bureau.

OF COURSE, WHILE Abby and Paolo were making the movie, I incurred a big parking mishap. We had just finished shooting a birth in Hoboken, New Jersey. I had driven there in a hurry, with Abby and Paolo as passengers, and parked quickly, thinking that we were pressed for time based on the doula's report. It turned out we had more time than I originally thought, but I didn't realize that when we were parking. When we came out to go home, I saw a yellow boot around my right front tire. I thought, *What the fuck? No!*

I looked at the instructional paper that is conveniently attached to the boot. To have the boot removed, a payment is required, and it would take time for someone to come remove it. After I dialed the number on the paper, the woman put me on hold. As I waited and listened to a looped recorded message, the voice on it said something that gave me pause — something about it costing $185 to get the boot taken off. I hung up, figuring I could always call back, and checked to see whether I could remove the boot myself. I quickly discovered the boot wasn't even firmly attached to my tire! I went back into the corner bodega to let the film crew know that I had resolved the problem and we could be on our way.

We drove out of the boot and left it behind on the street. But oh boy, did I have to pay for that injustice. For a month afterward, Hitomi, my assistant, dodged phone calls from Hoboken's Parking Violations Bureau reporting that we were going to be charged for the boot since we had taken it off and left it there. All of a sudden the boot was now my responsibility, and apparently it cost $500. Thank God for Althea, a Jersey City mom who had worked as an archivist for the ACLU. I got a lawyer's name from her.

There was more car trouble. The day I went to see the lawyer, my car's engine died on the Tappan Zee Bridge, and I had to rent a car to make it to my appointment. I kept it until my car was fixed so I had wheels in the event that I would be paged.

I watched and listened as the lawyer effortlessly discussed my case on the phone, saying there was no way that this petite woman, a nurse, whom he was looking right at, had removed the boot herself. I went to court, and the case was dismissed. Considering the importance of the work I do, I hate that I still have to deal with these petty agendas. In any case, I have always had a feeling that if I'm honest and stick to my guns, the truth will prevail, as it did in this circumstance. Come to think of it, I kind of wish this scene had wound up in the movie. Who knows? It might have helped me in my quest to get midwives special license plates.

※

CHAPTER 14

The Tables Turn

LOT HAPPENED AS the film progressed. Ricki swooped in and decided to take over the production and, hence, the funding of the film from the original sponsor, the Discovery Channel's health division. I was actually happy about that, even though it meant the film had a smaller budget. Freedom from any network, I was sure, would protect us from any biases and agendas.

When Discovery was still involved and there was more money for shooting, Abby and Paolo were trying to put in slices of my personal life. They filmed me swimming at the Sol Goldman Y — my favorite exercise routine, and something I make sure I do a few times a week. That was weird. I have never seen the footage and would probably really enjoy seeing myself swim. There was a plan to film me dancing salsa on Sunday nights, but that never materialized. I wasn't too upset about that, though. I do like to keep some of my life private.

The biggest thing to happen during filming was that Abby got pregnant. I don't think I found her unexpected pregnancy at all surprising. I know that different women prepare for birth in different ways. I would speculate that maybe for Abby, being so close to birth all the time let her get all the information that her journalist's soul might have needed to feel comfortable embracing the journey toward motherhood. I have learned in my work that the portal opens when the time is right.

Abby seemed to feel privileged to have the access she did, and that made it important for her to use the film to help women see inside the various birth options available to them. In a way, Abby became a spokesperson for those who wouldn't automatically seek out a homebirth when first becoming pregnant — about 99 percent of women.

Movie spoiler alert! Abby had to have a C-section because her baby was breech and preterm. One of the few issues I have with the movie is that some of the information surrounding Abby's delivery is not as clear as it should be. This lack of clarity has the potential to perpetuate the message that midwives aren't thorough clinicians. Moviegoers all express confusion about Abby's labor. They can't tell how long we were at home, why we were at home, and what the plan was. But I know and knew then the answers to all of these concerns. In fact I was directing that scene, yet it looks like I'm just along for the ride. I was told by a colleague that one of the doctors I work with regularly mistakenly thought that Abby was 40 weeks pregnant with a 3-pound, 5-ounce baby instead of being five weeks premature. This misconception insinuates that the baby was dangerously rescued from starvation. But Abby was in preterm labor with a baby in the breech position. No one for a minute, especially not me, fantasized that we would be proceeding with a birth at home under these circumstances. The DVD features outtakes that make all of this information clear, and that is definitely compensatory.

I also wish that there were some scenes of me listening to the baby's heart rate in labor, because I do it all the time. It is an essential part of making sure the baby is not in distress. Showing this would have proven that proceeding at home is indeed safe. Families choosing homebirth need to know that we do not forego checking on the baby while the mother is in labor. Some women who have come in to consult with me after seeing the film have felt much better when I elucidated this point.

All that said, while some doctors who see the movie may not be converted to midwifery proponents, the film is excellent and spells out many of the issues midwives face. It has begun to open people's eyes and to educate many mothers-to-be about the breadth of their choices. It also helps other midwives to join us in our cause and to feel re-energized about our work and the future of midwifery.

I am grateful for the film because it shows women there's another viable way to give birth besides at the hospital. It opens up the dialogue about homebirth. The movie is already making a difference — all of the homebirth midwives in New York City have their phones ringing off their hooks. They're getting calls from women who are finally tuning into their own instincts and rethinking their options instead of unconditionally trusting the hospital experience. The unarticulated has been articulated, and this is giving mothers the confidence to trust their inner voice.

Not only are pregnant women hearing the message, but caregivers are, too. Nearly three months after the release of *The Business of Being Born,* I had an emergent transfer to Elmhurst Hospital in Queens, my first in many months. Everything felt different from my last emergent transfer in Queens, where we lamented Sarah's unnecessary episiotomy.

This time, we were met with three lovely female residents who assured Anne, the mom, after she cried, "You're not going to cut me, are you?" that her baby was crowning nicely and there was no episiotomy necessary. I was perplexed that we were met with such respect and acceptance. Then one of the residents asked me to come out into the hallway. She introduced herself and shook my hand and told me that she and her colleagues had seen the movie just a few days earlier. I couldn't help but wonder, had the tables really begun to turn?

BEING INVOLVED WITH the movie and seeing the end product has made me hopeful about the future. That hope, in turn, has helped me to focus my energy on some of my ideas. I have a vision for a larger practice that fosters teamwork among several midwives. As it is now, a handful of successful yet small homebirth practices are each run by an individual midwife. This is what I have been doing for the past 12 years, and I am pretty sure that we can't advance without expanding beyond that model. We need teamwork. Many believe that starting a new midwife-run birthing center is the solution, but I don't want to be involved in a situation where, once again, institutional protocols govern clinical management to the detriment of individualized care.

I've taken the first baby steps (no pun intended) toward my new vision by inviting others to participate in my practice in a way that I perceive as beneficial for all. I knew that when the movie came out, many women might become inspired and want to try a homebirth, so I began figuring out a way to cope with a potentially increased demand without compromising all of the traits that make my practice so unique in terms of personal attention and devotion. And then, on cue, as if through divine grace, people began appearing to fill the roles I had imagined.

Kate, my longtime apprentice, started venting on a regular basis about how hard it was to watch women give birth at the hospital where she worked, in spite of the fact that it has a birth center. So I came up with a plan. Currently there is no setting where wannabe homebirth nurse-midwives can learn the trade from someone with experience. They have to work in hospitals to get their feet wet. But in effect, no one learning in a hospital gets practice in labor management that is anything other than standard. This makes it hard to start a private practice with confidence. A midwife is left to start on her own, pushing the boundaries and learning from experience. Since I had already done this with success, I figured that my practice could offer the opportunity for young aspiring midwives to learn the ways of homebirth.

I've now hired Kate, an RN, and also Tania, a Peruvian midwife who returned to New York specifically to do homebirth, since the political climate in Peru is not nearly as warm as it is here. These women will be midwife assistants in a model that will resemble the Dutch system, meaning that they will be involved in prenatal, birth, and postpartum care of my patients. I feel good about working with these two women whose work I know and whose personalities I'm familiar with.

My intention is to start Manhattan's first home delivery service predicated on incorporating community. I want the moms to get to know one another. This sort of maternal community can be a great way for women to quell their fears. They can lean on one another and not feel so alone in their "radical" choice of homebirth. I see this larger practice eventually being housed in a building with spaces for lectures, classes, and fun social gatherings — some for midwives, some for moms, and some for both. I hope that we can also create a maternity spa, where moms can get prenatal bodywork of all kinds.

My blueprint for the future is this: My practice will be staffed by me, two midwife assistants, and a midwife-in-training whose births I will attend to ensure her confidence, and that of her patients, until she's ready to launch a practice of her own. Other members of my team would be a resident photographer, an acupuncturist, a hypnobirther, and a lactation consultant. Featuring these people in my practice would facilitate my moms' searches for good referrals that I can vouch for since I have watched them practice over the years. And truly, each one of them brings special gifts.

Then to add some fun, we have already begun group prenatal visits where we delve into pregnancy- and childbirth-related subjects, such as hypnobirthing's effects on labor. We're also going to help women just enjoy pregnancy by inviting them to come and participate in things like belly casting and holistic beauty treatments.

My idea is to help women go though this important psychological transformation with excellent support from professionals and from expectant mothers just like themselves. That support is one of the key missing pieces to the homebirth process. If we had that, we could help make more women, and then more doctors, and then our culture as a whole, more comfortable with homebirth. The film got the ball rolling, and I'm determined to keep it rolling.

I AM ALSO STILL HOPING that my brief alliance with Hollywood will get me a stint on *Pimp My Ride*. And, of course, special license plates.

Perhaps there was temporary karmic justice in the beneficent parking situation on the night of the movie's premiere. Of course, the night when my 15 minutes of fame began, duty called. Things like that just reconfirm my instinct that I am better suited for a life of service than life in the spotlight. But for once, the parking gods were firmly on my side.

It had been an especially busy day. In addition to my rounds of prenatal house calls — circling the streets of New York City in search of parking spaces and hauling my doctor's bag and backpack up and down countless flights of steps in various patients' apartment buildings — I'd had some serious primping to tend to. There was the visit to the seamstress to get my Vera Wang gown (a $30 score on Bluefly.com) fitted and a hair appointment.

At 6:30 PM, with an hour left until the 7:30 red carpet call, it seemed as if I were actually going to have time to kick back. Then my pager went off. An expectant first-time mother in the West Village needed me. She was having contractions. *Why now?* I grumbled to myself. I knew in my bones she was in very early labor. But more than that, I knew in my heart that she needed me to show up.

With my hair and makeup done, I threw on my shiny gown and jumped in the car. Eight blocks down Avenue B, I made a right on Third Street, then flew across town. As I pulled up to the expectant parents' building, I was met with the New York City version of divine intervention: someone was right then pulling out of a prime parking spot, one that I could keep for the rest of the evening. Ironically — and fortunately — the parents, a young lesbian couple, lived just around the corner from the theater where the premiere was being held. After checking out the mother and baby and getting a handle on the situation — she was in latent labor, and the baby wouldn't be born for two days — I was able to just make it to the premiere.

✳

ACKNOWLEDGMENTS

THERE ARE MANY PEOPLE without whom this book would not have been possible, and I extend my gratitude to them all.

Many thanks to Sari Botton, my memoir midwife, for providing a framework for my thoughts and for helping me find my voice.

To my savvy editor, Shannon Berning at Kaplan Publishing, without whose vision this book would not have come about.

And to my agent, Jim Flynn, whose guidance and support have been invaluable.

I am forever grateful to Ricki Lake and Abby Epstein, producer and director, respectively, of the eye-opening documentary *The Business of Being Born*. Thank you, ladies, for including me in that wonderful film and for helping to foster a positive image of homebirth. And thanks to Paolo Netto, the fantastic cinematographer.

Thank you, Miriam Schwarzschild, for so very much: for being a brave trailblazer in the field of home midwifery, for being a mentor, for being a great friend, for being my midwife, and for referring Ricki to me when you decided to turn down the opportunity to be in her film.

Thanks also to all my other esteemed midwifery colleagues, including Sylvie Blaustein, Valeriana Pascua-Masbeck, Joan Bryson, and Michelle Handleman; the many wonderful doulas I work with, especially Jenna Hutchens and Sarah Pancake; and the highly evolved doctors who collaborate with us so beautifully, including Jacques Moritz, Eden Fromberg, Franz Margono, John Maggio, and Donald Matheson. And of course, thank you to my incredible assistants, Hitomi Matarese and Katie Baker.

Thanks, as well, to Priscilla Young Rogers, who always helps me find the light of my path during times of chaos and darkness — and who has helped me navigate some of the darkest days with hope and humility.

Thanks to Daphne Beal for her honest and positive portrayal of her homebirth with me in the November 2007 issue of *Vogue*. And to all my other amazing, powerful moms and their beautiful families, whose trust I have had the privilege to win.

My own family has provided such incredible inspiration and support in many different ways. Thank you, Mom, wherever you are, for making motherhood look like it was both fun and fulfilling and for setting a wonderful example as a person working in service to others. Thank you, Dad, for instilling in me a love and respect for nature and for encouraging me always to follow my star. My big sister, Kim, has been an incredible leader and guide for me through many of life's passages, and I will always be grateful. And thanks to all of my sisters (and my surrogate sisters, the Riccardos), I learned what sisterhood is about. Thanks to Karin, my very first au pair, who with her amazing love allowed me to trust another human being with the care of my son for the first time.

My thanks, too, to Geoff and Goussy and Omi for being my partners in parenthood; without them, I wouldn't be able to answer to the calls of this demanding profession. And above all, thank you, Liam, for making me a mommy, for being an amazing kid, and for sacrificing all you do for a higher calling.

READER'S GROUP GUIDE

1. In *Labor of Love*, Muhlhahn's parents taught her "that nature's systems are often better than those created by humans." What are some examples of this idea that Muhlhahn's parents pointed out to her? What are some examples that Muhlhahn learned as a midwife? How did this realization impact her career?

2. Muhlhahn writes, "I have come to know god in my own way and on my own terms, through the work I do." What are the experiences, as a midwife and even before she became a midwife, that catalyzed her spirituality? How does she define "god"?

3. How does Muhlhahn's personal spirituality come up against the Catholic tradition in which her mother was raised (but which her mother rejected)? Does she prefer other religious traditions? In what ways did she collide with Catholicism professionally?

4. "When emergency situations arose, I was able to pull myself together, take control, and keep everyone else calm, too," Muhlhahn writes. This is a trait that Muhlhahn

demonstrates throughout her life and career. Where does it come from—that is, how does she develop it? Is it a necessary quality for the work that she does? Does she ever describe moments when she was unable to stay in control during a crisis?

5. Muhlhahn discusses her self-image several times, saying, for example, "What I met in France was a less objectified version of women, that was at the same time less prudish than what I had known at home." How did this exposure affect her subsequent life and career? When she was pregnant, Muhlhahn writes that she wore bikinis and midriff-revealing tops; were these clothing choices influenced by her time in Europe?

6. When she was in college, Muhlhahn says she realized that "I wanted to help others concretely, person-to-person, face-to-face." Many of the decisions she made in her life came from this focus on the fundamental purpose of her life, the desire to understand what truly matters. How does she seek out this purpose? What are her criteria for what is important? What incorrect routes does she take? What helps her settle on midwifery as her calling?

7. Muhlhahn described several people who mentored her as she learned what she had to know for her career; among them are Johanna in Oregon, Melinda in Texas, Mae Chin at the North Central Bronx Hospital, and Miriam Schwartzchild at Columbia Presbyterian. What did she learn from each of these people?

8. Another type of experience that somehow aided her quest was what she calls a "cosmic kick in the pants," which she defines as being "faced with some horrible humiliation or other formidable challenge [that causes] me to question who and what I am." One such example is when she was not given the job of charge nurse at Columbia Presbyterian's Allen Pavillion. What are others that she describes? How does Muhlhahn hold on to her passion, even in the face of such setbacks?

9. One of her tools for challenging the conventional wisdom of the hospital where she worked was index cards with research and case histories written on them. Muhlhahn would take out these cards whenever her decisions were being disregarded. Was this an effective tactic against medical orthodoxy?

10. Muhlhahn mentions "the flip-flopping of obstetrical absolutes," how conventional medical wisdom about delivery seems to change on a regular basis, and a conviction one year is a superstition the next. What are some of the examples she mentions? Are there any that she doesn't mention but which could be included?

11. According to Muhlhahn, with a "rule book that keeps changing as new authorities keep coming forward, the entire pregnant population is in a neurotic state, always confused about what to do and eat and whether or not they can or should exercise. This sends them in search of experts possessing temporary truths that do nothing to render them confident in their pregnancies." What other reasons does she give for

the way expecting mothers are directed toward doctors and hospitals rather than midwives and home delivery?

12. At several points in *Labor of Love*, Muhlhahn refers to birth as a journey and discusses a less clinical, more emotional or spiritual aspect to pregnancy and birth to which she tries to remain aware. How is birth like a psychological journey—what is the destination? What does Muhlhahn think women can take from their births, besides bringing a new child into the world?